'Few issues are as pressing fo[...]
approach to power and lead[...]
on it as Marcus Honeysett. [...]
for our times. I am confident it will help [...]
safety and health.'
Sam Allberry, pastor and author

'A really important book that contains warning signs for all in Christian leadership. I pray that it will make a significant impact in enabling healthier leadership in our churches.'
Gavin Calver, CEO, Evangelical Alliance

'What an important book! This is a must-read, must-think-about, must-act-on essential read for all church leaders – and members. Marcus writes wisely, courageously, searchingly and humbly. He keeps shining the light of Christ's grace into the dark corners of our leadership lives. It should lead all of us to be more repentant, more believing and more humble servants of the Lord and people.

'I think his description of what should be Bible-based, transparent, legitimate and boundaried church leadership is spot on. This book must not be ignored by any servant of the Lord.'
Dr Ray Evans, FIEC Leadership Consultant and a pastor at Grace Community Church, Bedford

'Being concerned for how Christian leaders lead and the potential for power abuses is neither a passing fad nor capitulation to some external agendas. It is a profoundly biblical and godly concern and Marcus Honeysett has written such a helpful and down-to-earth introduction to some of the key issues. Many of us feel immobilized by fears of getting things wrong but, in this book, we find practical wisdom and helpful questions, especially in identifying stages along the slippery slope to abuse. This will be invaluable both for leaders and those they lead.'
Mark Meynell, Director, Europe and Caribbean, Langham Preaching

'Marcus understands the subtleties involved within the power dynamics of leadership and life in the local church. The book will save you from simplistic understanding of why power is wielded poorly and enable you to act thoughtfully and prayerfully to deal not only with the worst excesses, but also any creeping slippage in your own heart. I would certainly give every newcomer to pastoral ministry a copy but, if you are already leading, I would suggest you read it prayerfully with your leadership team and reap the benefits in your local church.'
Andy Peck, host of *The Leadership Show*, Premier Christian Radio

'In a season where we are only too aware of the clay feet of some of our Christian leaders, Marcus's timely book speaks with compassion, integrity and a deep knowledge of his subject area. While an admittedly sobering read, this wise and practical book perceptively outlines the early warning signs of the misuse of power in a leadership context. Engaging with biblical material and real-life experiences, *Powerful Leaders* will be a vital resource for all kinds of leaders and churches who wish to pursue godly wisdom, accountability and integrity in leadership.'
The Revd Dr Hannah Steele, Director, St Mellitus College, London

'The power dimension in relationships, unrecognized for most of my ministry, is now centre stage. Marcus Honeysett has thought deeply about the issue and provided a forensic analysis of what can go wrong, based on a wide range of experiences. He has also provided an encouraging, practical guide to both avoiding problems and putting them right when they occur. Reading the book will help every leader to look in the mirror. The key is then not to forget what we have seen.'
Derek Tidball, theologian, writer and previous Principal, London School of Theology

'The author introduces the reader to what is a complex and challenging issue in the church today. He helpfully identifies five factors by which a leader can review or be reviewed within any context. The section on leaders understanding and reflecting on their leadership provides good questions and thoughts on how a leader with genuine concern to lead with humility and dependence can do a self-appraisal. There are many helpful insights in this book, which will be a useful tool.'
Dianne Tidball, ex-president of The Baptist Union, Baptist Regional Minister, and Deputy Chair, Hope in Action

'Having read Marcus Honeysett's fine book, several observations come to mind. It is insightful, wise, thorough, sensitive and compassionate; a careful handling of a delicate theme by someone with genuine care for the body of Christ, avoiding accusation but arguing constructively for paths of peace and security.'
Terry Virgo, founder of Newfrontiers and author of *God's Treasured Possession*

POWERFUL LEADERS?

POWERFUL LEADERS?

When church leadership goes wrong
and how to prevent it

Marcus Honeysett

INTER-VARSITY PRESS
36 Causton Street, London SW1P 4ST, England
Email: ivp@ivpbooks.com
Website: www.ivpbooks.com

First published 2022

British Library Cataloguing-in-Publication Data
A catalogue record for this book is available from the British Library.

ISBN: 978–1–78974–322–7
eBook ISBN: 978–1–78974–345–6

Set in Minion Pro 10.25/13.75pt
Typeset in Great Britain by CRB Associates, Potterhanworth, Lincolnshire
Printed and bound in Great Britain by Clays Ltd, Elcograf S.p.A.

Produced on paper from sustainable sources

Inter-Varsity Press publishes Christian books that are true to the Bible and that communicate the gospel, develop discipleship and strengthen the church for its mission in the world.

IVP originated within the Inter-Varsity Fellowship, now the Universities and Colleges Christian Fellowship, a student movement connecting Christian Unions in universities and colleges throughout Great Britain, and a member movement of the International Fellowship of Evangelical Students. Website: www.uccf.org.uk. That historic association is maintained, and all senior IVP staff and committee members subscribe to the UCCF Basis of Faith.

Contents

Contents

Introduction

This is what the Sovereign LORD says: Woe to the shepherds of Israel who only take care of themselves! Should not shepherds take care of the flock? You eat the curds, clothe yourselves with the wool and slaughter the choice animals, but you do not take care of the flock. You have not strengthened the weak or healed the sick or bound up the injured ... You have ruled them harshly and brutally.
(Ezekiel 34:2–4)

The evangelistic youth service was rapidly approaching, but Greg the minister was worried. It wasn't that the youth were actively voting with their feet but there was a decided lack of enthusiasm. Two weeks before, he decided to pop into the youth meeting to encourage them. 'Come on, everyone. Let's think now about who we are going to invite,' he said. 'You don't want the event to bomb, do you? It would be very sad if we had to cancel it. You do want your friends to hear about Jesus, don't you?' The youth all looked at their shoes, uneasily.

A couple of days later Greg was approached by Sally, a concerned parent, who said that her daughter was in floods of tears because she couldn't think how to invite people and wondered if the success of the event and the salvation of her friends depended on her doing something she felt unable to do. Several others apparently felt the same. Sally gently asked Greg whether he had put too much pressure on the youth. Greg had never thought about power dynamics when he was with the youth group. Considering himself easy-going and likeable, he could scarcely imagine that anyone would interpret his relational encouragement to evangelize as undue pressure. He didn't *think* he had abused his power or position. He had no intention of using the youth to make his vision happen, but had he inadvertently crossed a line and used the power of his position or his winsome personality to coerce young people into doing something they didn't want to do?

Mapping the slippery slope

This is a book about what happens when Christian leadership goes wrong. Today's culture has become deeply sensitive to issues of power imbalance, misuse of authority and manipulation. The story above is a relatively innocuous example of a situation in which there is no intention to discourage, but also no thought has been given to the relational power dynamics at play.

At the other end of the spectrum, far more serious abuses of power and position (both historical and contemporary) have recently come to light in a variety of Christian settings, in which leaders have misused their authority, not to feed the flock of God but rather to feed on it. Examples range from patterns of hurtful leadership behaviour to harassment, coercive and dominating leadership, and even criminal physical and/or sexual abuse. Names that used to be held in respect are now synonymous with something else.

In this book I attempt to step back to address issues of authority and power through a somewhat more objective framework. However, it is important to say at the outset that the issues are profoundly personal and intensely painful. I have been deeply saddened by hearing victims and survivors of manipulative or bullying leaders describe how bonds of trust have been broken, emotional lifelong scars have been inflicted, and lives have been devastated by the inability or refusal of churches, tribes and denominations to deal with those who misuse their power and position. I am incredibly grateful to the many people who have shared painful stories, experiences and concerns with me, and have no doubt there are more whose stories have yet to be heard and for whom justice has yet to be served. I know also, from first-hand experience, the pain and personal cost of being on the wrong end of coercive and manipulative leaders. While this doesn't give me any greater right to comment on the painful situations that others face, I hope readers won't feel that what follows comes from some disinterested armchair theorist.

My aim is modest. I hope to sketch a map of the slippery slope of power – the path that runs from good intentions, via lack of accountability and transparency, down into manipulation and self-serving, all the way to the most serious abuses – and put up some 'turn back' signs. It isn't intended to be a comprehensive treatment. Rather it is a first word that I hope may provide a diagnosis of common symptoms to increase awareness and suggest some basic first aid. While I will discuss some of the *worst* abuses of power and position, I spend more time exploring the *first* abuses that set leaders on the slippery slope. My prayer is that describing the issues will help us spot if we or others are in danger of heading down the slope – God willing, before we damage other people or bring disrepute on Christ and the gospel.

No doubt a small minority become Christian leaders actively seeking ungodly opportunities to exercise power over others. They are, deliberately and intentionally, the wolves described by Ezekiel. Terrifyingly, they are even worse than wolves in sheep's clothing – they are wolves in *shepherd's* clothing.[1] From the outset they are coercive predators, in it for themselves. However, I believe the great majority of leaders don't deliberately set out to abuse power and position. Nevertheless, some do despite their initial good intentions. Misuse of power, as we shall see, might not be intended to harm, but lack of intention doesn't remove culpability. The heart is deceitful, and we are never fully aware of our own motives.

That leaders can abuse power without realizing it, either through ignorance or self-deceit, should make us all the more serious and

---

1 The metaphor of wolves in shepherd's clothing is not mine, but I have been unable to find a clear single origin for it.

self-reflective about our use of it. As in the case of vicar Greg, it is common for leaders to miss warning signs. Greg's negative impact on the youth was quite unintentional, but his being oblivious didn't make it any less real. And if leaders can misuse position and power unintentionally (as well as very deliberately, as we shall see), churches can equally be blind to it. They rely heavily on trust in leaders and are often unaware of where the limits on leader authority ought to lie.

No Christian leader – no leader of any kind – is immune from the dangers of misuse of power and position. Which frustrated leader has never thought something like, 'If I could remove that person and replace them with someone who would be more supportive, I could actually do what needs to be done, and the church would probably not question it if I did'?

Asking the right questions

In what follows, the vital questions are: could I be in danger of misusing power and position? Could our church? How would I know? Would anyone have the courage to tell me, and how would I respond if they did? Are the structures around me sufficiently transparent and helpful to stop me if I am unknowingly on a trajectory towards shipwreck? I pray that what follows will help you and your church bring these things into the light.

I am keenly aware of the difficulty of writing on this subject from within a Christian tribe. It is next to impossible to identify one's own blind spots. Without doubt there are evangelical power structures, and I am a (very minor) part of them. Like every leader, I am aware that I have not always unfailingly exercised authority wisely and kindly myself. Furthermore, the issues we are going to examine play out differently in different Christian cultures, tribes and denominations, according to their respective understandings of how leadership authority is assigned and exercised. My own tribe is UK independent evangelical, and I have some experience of the world of mission agencies. I am very grateful for insights from Anglican friends, but have little personal experience of how issues of misuse of power work in episcopal or synodical settings. If the book is to be useful to you, you will need to translate some of what follows in the light of your own situation.

What this book is not

After a lot of thought, I have decided not to discuss the particularities of high-profile cases or individuals. This may distress some readers by giving the impression that I am minimizing the seriousness of leader malpractice or, even worse, covering up for abusers. Nothing could be further from my intention. My hope is to provide a framework that is relevant to specific situations in the public eye at the time of writing, but also more generally. The pen portraits in the book are fictional composites, but all illustrate real issues I have encountered over the years. Additionally, I have provided links in the bibliography to several reports in the public domain regarding specific cases, and I recommend reading these alongside this book.

Furthermore, at points I seek to understand and address some of the pressures of ministry that might play into leaders going bad. I realize that this may be uncomfortable for readers who are victims or survivors of power abuse. This is in no way intended to excuse or justify any form of harmful leadership, undermine victims or qualify their need for justice, but I recognize that it could be interpreted as explaining away wicked behaviour. There is nothing as painful as making public revelations of abuse, at great personal cost, only to be further hurt by feeling that someone is downplaying them. My hope is that careful investigation of complexities will help us improve our understanding and make us more able and willing to repent and change when abuses of position and power come to light – and ideally before they do.

Introduction

This is not a technical book. I have no expertise in safeguarding or legal matters. Rather, it is simply observations from twenty-five years in Christian ministry, the last fifteen of which have centred on mentoring church leaders.[2] It is paid leaders I have most in mind, but my hope is that it will be helpful to leaders and church officers across the warp and weft of wider church life, to leaders in Christian agencies, to those considering or preparing for vocational ministry and those who train them.

I am extremely grateful to those who have shared their stories and concerns. Many have offered suggestions and corrections that have greatly improved the book. Special thanks are due to my wife Ros, my Living Leadership colleague Paul Coulter, and Caleb Woodbridge and Tom Creedy at IVP. All errors, of course, are mine.

---

2 At the time of writing, others are also reflecting very helpfully on similar themes but with somewhat different approaches. To mention just two, for victim-centred thinking informed by a deep understanding of trauma I highly recommend the work of psychologist Diane Langberg; and for pastoral reflections on leadership and personality, readers would benefit greatly from the writing of professor and counsellor Chuck DeGroat.

Part 1

BIBLICAL PATTERNS OF HEALTHY LEADERSHIP

1

Servant leadership
for the good of others

[Jesus] asked them, 'What were you arguing about on the road?' But they kept quiet because on the way they had argued about who was the greatest. Sitting down, Jesus called the Twelve and said, 'If anyone wants to be first, he must be the very last, and the servant of all.' He took a little child and had him stand among them.
(Mark 9:33–36a)

I wonder if you have ever attended a conference or watched a video online in which a passionate and motivated speaker has enthused about the successes of their church or movement. You were inspired by accounts of people being saved, baptized and discipled, and were challenged by the vision, strategies and tough choices the leader had made.

We are easily drawn in by energy, drive, charisma and what seems like success. But how can we tell if what we are seeing is healthy, biblical leadership? How can we look beyond charisma to character and submission to Scripture? And if you yourself are that leader up on stage, how can you ensure you are modelling healthy leadership?

Before we explore the trajectory that leads away from healthy biblical leadership and into danger, we first need to establish a plumb line: what does the New Testament say about authentic, healthy Christian leadership?

Disciples getting it wrong

James and John asked Jesus to give them the most glorious places in his kingdom. In return Jesus gave them an extended telling-off for wanting to exercise leadership in the same way as the world. '[The] rulers of the Gentiles lord it over them,' he said. 'Not so with you.' He presented himself as their model to emulate: 'even the Son of Man did not come to be served, but to serve, and to give his life as a ransom for many' (Mark 10:42–43, 45). The world says that leadership is about power, status, accomplishment, climbing the ladder and being the boss. Leaders are at the top of the pile. The fact that James and John's request is recorded shows that Christians are far from immune from this temptation.

For several years I taught a course in church leadership, for which I read much of the work published in the UK over a thirty-year period. By far the most common definition of leadership was 'leadership is influence', a definition you will struggle to find in the Bible. It is a pragmatic, secular definition, baptized and used in the church, and labelled therefore as 'Christian leadership', not dissimilar to the role and skill set of a CEO or company director, only exercised in a Christian context.

However, Christian leadership is of a completely different kind. We have a different goal: God being glorified through people coming to Jesus and becoming worshipping disciples. We have different motivation, power, methods and character. Leadership is not merely the exercise of influence or a set of skills and competencies.

Leadership is servanthood

Of course, the other main definition of leadership is servanthood. But even then, it is reasonably rare to find it explained and explored in leadership books rather than just assumed. Let's examine a few passages to help us put flesh on the bones of what 'servant leadership' means.

1 What is Christian leadership?

Christian leadership is a spiritual gift. 'We have different gifts according to the grace given us. If a man's gift is . . . leadership, let him govern diligently' (Romans 12:6, 8).

In 1 Corinthians 12:7 the spiritual gifts are described as manifestations of the Holy Spirit for the common good. A manifestation is a showing or demonstration of the Holy Spirit. He gives gifts to Christians so that God will be seen. The apostle Peter expands on how grace gifts from God (of which every Christian has at least one) are to be used: 'Each one should use whatever gift he has received to serve others, faithfully administering God's grace in its various forms' (1 Peter 4:10).

Spiritual gifts then, including leadership, are given to each believer, not for ourselves but for serving others, in the common good. When we use our spiritual gifts to serve in this way, we are stewards of God's grace. Peter highlights the overall purpose: 'so that in all things God may be praised through Jesus Christ. To him be the glory and the power for ever and ever. Amen' (1 Peter 4:11).

2 What is the point of Christian leadership?

The point of Christian leadership is to build up the body in maturity, love and effectiveness. We serve, stewarding grace gifts from God, so that he is known, worshipped and glorified through Jesus. The context in which leadership is exercised is the church, which is God's worshipping, witnessing community, the body of Christ. In Ephesians 4 we discover that 'to each one of us grace has been given as Christ apportioned it' (verse 7). 'It was he who gave some to be apostles, some to be prophets, some to be evangelists, and some to be pastors and teachers, to prepare God's people for works of service' (verses 11–12).

God gives leaders to help everyone else to use their own gifts in his service. The aim is that 'the body of Christ may be built up until we all reach unity in the faith and in the knowledge of the Son of God and become mature, attaining to the whole measure of the fulness of Christ' (verses 12–13).

This maturity is experienced by not being blown around by false teaching: 'Then we will no longer be infants . . . blown here and there by every wind of teaching and by the cunning and craftiness of men in their deceitful scheming' (verse 14) and by the body growing in love and doing its work effectively:

> Instead, speaking the truth in love, we will in all things grow up into him who is the Head, that is, Christ. From him the whole body, joined and held together by every supporting ligament, grows and builds itself up in love, as each part does its work.
> (verses 15–16)

The point of Christian leadership is to shepherd the body, and all the disciples within it, to play their part in God's great purposes. Leaders are given to equip and nurture all the disciples in their ministries, not to do all the ministry of the church for them.

3 How do Christian leaders do this?

Christian leaders shepherd the body by working with people for their progress and joy in the faith. The apostle Paul told the church in Philippi what he wanted to do upon his release from prison: 'I will continue with all of you for your progress and joy in the faith, so that through my being with you again your joy in Christ Jesus will overflow on account of me' (Philippians 1:25–26). His aim is that they will glory abundantly in Jesus, being full of joy in him. Christian joy is the experience of gladness or happiness, not in plans or possessions or ambitions, but in God. When we become Christians, we are saved into a relationship in which he gives his joy to us. In John 15:11, Jesus tells the disciples to remain in him, and thereby in the love of the Father, so that his joy may be in them and their joy may be complete. The core focus of Christian leaders, therefore, is that disciples will know and enjoy God as they obey and follow Jesus.

The heartbeat of all discipleship and all leadership is the joy of the Lord, of which experiencing his grace is the wellspring. The Bible is clear that the joy of the Lord is our strength (Nehemiah 8:10). And yet it can come as a surprise, even to seasoned leaders. One church leader told me, 'I have never seen that my job is to be a worker who helps other people overflow with joy in God. That revolutionizes everything.' When a church is full of joy in God it is easy to see why it attracts people to Christ. Similarly, when it isn't, we can see easily why there is little attraction.

James and John got it wrong. Christian leaders are not Jesus' top generals. They are under-shepherds helping the flock enjoy and feed on God, out of which flows firm and secure faith: 'Not that we lord it over your faith, but we work with you for your joy, because it is by faith you stand firm' (2 Corinthians 1:24).

4 What does this look like in practice?

In practice this involves teaching, shepherding, modelling and spiritual parenting. The church in Thessalonica, whose founding provoked a riot (Acts 17:1–8), was a great source of joy to the apostle Paul, because they were imitators: 'You became imitators of us and of the Lord; in spite of severe suffering, you welcomed the message with the joy given by the Holy Spirit' (1 Thessalonians 1:6).

The modelling and example they received included hearing the gospel and witnessing leaders who were genuine (1 Thessalonians 2:5). Paul and his team were gentle and caring, encouraging like mothers (2:7), sharing their lives as well as the gospel (2:8). Like spiritual fathers they comforted, encouraged and urged the new disciples to live for God (2:11–12). All with the aim that God would make your love increase and overflow for each other and for everyone else, just as ours does for you. May he strengthen your hearts so that you will be blameless and holy in the presence of our God and Father when our Lord Jesus comes with all his holy ones.

(1 Thessalonians 3:12–13)

5 In what do authentic leaders boast?

Authentic Christian leaders boast in weakness, not strength. In 2 Corinthians 12, the apostle Paul talks about his famous 'thorn in the flesh'. We don't know what it was, but it was distressing and he pleaded three times with the Lord to take it away. The Lord did not remove it, but instead used it to teach him a vital lesson about grace, power and weakness: 'But he said to me, "My grace is sufficient for you, for my power is made perfect in weakness"' (verse 9). Note the connection between God's grace and power and Paul's weakness. It is when we are weak that God's power is manifest, not when we are strong. His grace is sufficient. Paul continues:

Therefore I will boast all the more gladly about my weaknesses, so that Christ's power may rest on me. That is why, for Christ's sake, I delight in weaknesses, in insults, in hardships, in persecutions, in difficulties. For when I am weak, then I am strong.
(verses 9–10)

The trouble for many of us as Christian leaders is that we simply don't like it! Or we think that our churches don't want it. Faced with a choice between apparently strong, resilient, visionary, resourceful leaders or weak but prayerful ones, we secretly think the church wants the first type. We can imagine that they won't want us if we delight in weakness. We can confuse confidence with competence, all the while neglecting character. Maybe we even fear that if we embrace weakness God might not honour it, and we will find ourselves both disempowered and no longer respected by the people we are meant to lead.

But this *is* authentic Christian leadership – encouraging, modelling, parenting, comforting, strengthening hearts in the Lord and, in our weakness, helping people to live lives worthy of God.

As we make and mature disciples, the aim, just as it was in Thessalonica, is that believers would know God and glory in Jesus, and would be full of joy given by the Holy Spirit, increasing in holiness, abounding in hope and overflowing in love. We long to see them welcome the gospel message with joy and base their lives on their hope in the risen Jesus, and then see the message ringing out from them.

One church leader told me in conversation: 'I thought I was appointed to do all the ministry. I was taught that only people ordained by a bishop have spiritual gifts.' It was no surprise that in his church he expected to do everything and for the congregation to act as consumers of his professional ministry. He had a theology of them *not* having spiritual gifts to use.

Another said: 'The pathology is such that churches can be set up not to equip each saint, but for the saints to remain at primary school level, with the pastors feeling good about themselves rather than helping them towards maturity.'

It is vital to get the foundations right. God gives leaders to the church to help all the disciples get involved with Christ and his cause, living lives worthy of the calling of God. Leaders are under-shepherds for the glory of God and for the good of his people, feeding his flock and spreading his fame. We serve churches so that God is glorified: 'For we do not preach ourselves, but Jesus Christ as Lord, and ourselves as your servants *for Jesus' sake*' (2 Corinthians 4:5, emphasis added).

Christian leadership is not foundationally about running a church or some activity within a church. Skills in organizing and running a church are important, but that's just a function. Being a servant of a church for the sake of the Lord means that everything leaders do is so that Jesus is exalted in their own lives and the lives of others. The heart of leadership is joining with the work of the Holy Spirit in forming Christ-besotted worshippers.

Putting it into practice

We have barely scratched the surface of the New Testament's teaching on leadership – let alone that of the whole of Scripture! One other passage that offers us some helpful direction in our own formation as leaders is 1 Timothy 3, which lays out clearly that Christ-like character and the ability to teach the gospel correctly are fundamental to practising leadership.

Four features in particular stand out in helping to ensure that leaders remain godly and avoid misuse of position and power. These are: accountability, plurality, transparency and embodiment in the local church community.[1]

1 Accountability

People should be tested before they can serve as leaders (1 Timothy 3:10). Churches and denominations will differ on what the legitimate mechanisms for scrutiny should be, but being appropriately accountable for both our personal walk of faith and our use of power and authority is vital.

This is not to say that leaders never make mistakes, sometimes bad ones, or that they never need to repent and seek forgiveness. Godly leaders should in fact be the chief repenters. As we will see, leaders

---

1   I'm grateful to an Anglican friend who pointed out that in denominational settings this maps nicely on to:
   • accountability to those in hierarchical authority above us;
   • plurality with peers in leadership alongside us;
   • transparency with every church member over whom our position confers some degree of authority.

who evade accountability or avoid evaluation stand in much greater danger of misusing power to excuse and cover up misjudgements, errors and sin. And leaders who are deeply embedded relationally in the community need to be carefully accountable so that they do not misuse the very relational capital and credibility that makes their ministry work.

2 Plurality

Leadership in the New Testament is resolutely plural and collegial. The picture is of shepherds acting together, not of lone rangers. Plurality alone doesn't ensure that leadership remains godly, of course. There is always the danger of an inner circle of mutually reinforcing controlling people. But the lone leader is in far greater danger than the one who shares with colleagues.

3 Transparency

Paul says that overseers must be above reproach. Elsewhere he tells Timothy to let people see his progress. He himself has allowed his own life to be an open book (2 Timothy 3:10). Christian leadership is not politics. It never stitches things up behind the scenes. It should be exercised visibly, in plain sight, so that people can have confidence they are not being manipulated:

> Rather, we have renounced secret and shameful ways; we do not use deception, nor do we distort the word of God. On the contrary, by setting forth the truth plainly we commend ourselves to every man's conscience in the sight of God.
> (2 Corinthians 4:2)

4 Embodiment in the church community

Leaders are models and examples, first in their families (1 Timothy 3:4) and then in the church (e.g. Philippians 2:19–30; 1 Timothy 4:12–16). My friend Gordon Dalzell says that leadership is an 'imprinting responsibility', like the imprint of an old signet ring on sealing wax. It is not merely a set of learnable, transferable skills that can be exercised with a life divorced from embodiment in the church community.

Leaders are spiritual parents in whose lives the effects of the gospel should be clearly visible and possible to emulate. How else can leaders encourage people to imitate them as they imitate Christ (1 Corinthians 11:1)? Leaders are not religious professionals carrying out a function while holding the community at arm's length. People should be able to see how they live before God, so they know how to do likewise: 'We loved you so much that we were delighted to share with you not only the gospel of God but our lives as well, because you had become so dear to us' (1 Thessalonians 2:8).

In Part 2 we will see how each of these four characteristics is key to trustworthiness and good practice, and how evading or avoiding them can easily turn into misuse of position and power. Before that, however, we need to consider how authority can be exercised in a healthy and godly manner.

2

Healthy authority

And Saul's son Jonathan went to David at Horesh and helped
him to find strength in God.
(1 Samuel 23:16)

Discipleship or coercion?

Once when I had been away from home for extended periods on
ministry trips, a good friend knocked on our front door, concerned.
She plucked up the courage to ask my wife if everything was OK in
our marriage, or whether my absence was suggesting something was
amiss. We explained my travels over a cup of tea and told her that we
were extremely grateful for her loving concern – and nothing was
amiss!

This highlighted for us that people have different expectations
and thresholds for what constitutes acceptable Christian discipleship, looking out for one another, accountability and the boundaries
of authentic church community. We were delighted that she had
asked, but realized that not everyone would be. I remember a leader
saying to me that he couldn't possibly ask questions about someone
else's personal walk with the Lord, because he wouldn't welcome
being asked the same questions back. I once told a non-Christian
friend how valuable I found accountability to other Christians
and he replied, 'That's extremely strange. Nobody except Christians would find that degree of involvement from other people in
their lives a positive thing.' What I welcome and would not live
without could possibly be interpreted by others as intrusion or even
coercion.

Our culture is highly individualistic and places a high value on expressive individualism, affirming every individual in their self-defined identity. In this context, even historical Christian teachings and theology are open to being interpreted as coercive power dynamics. Submission to God and his lordship, repenting of sin and turning to Christ, obeying God's word and belonging to him, biblical ethics, church discipline, any asymmetry in the roles of men and women, and obeying Christian leaders are easily interpreted as unhealthy and damaging power imbalances.

How do we practise authority, discipleship, even church discipline, on the basis of servant leadership? How can we avoid these being coercive and harmful, first of all in reality and second in perception? The threshold between healthy exercise of authority and being domineering may not always be easy to discern.[1] Unless expectations are very clear at the point of joining a church (and repeatedly restated thereafter), it can be hard to evaluate once inside whether authority is being used healthily or not. As we will see, it is vital to have clear and transparent structures and mechanisms for leader accountability.

Leaders have power and authority – and rightly so

All leaders have some power resources at their disposal. Whether a little or a lot, all have some and it is right they do. Without it a parent cannot discipline a child, an employer cannot insist on standards of work, a teacher can't teach and a trainer cannot correct an apprentice.

By 'power' I mean having the *ability* to act, and by 'authority' I mean having the *right* to act. Christian leaders have power and authority by a combination of two main means:

---

1 These questions can be particularly acute in the case of entrepreneurial founder-leaders or evangelists, who often have the robust and forceful personalities necessary for creating something from scratch.

- The formal authority that attaches to their role and position.
- The relational capital that they acquire as they serve people and gain their trust. Some personality types more naturally garner trust and social credibility.

Some leaders have additional power because they occupy platforms or have wider influence in a denomination, tribe or culture. We will explore some of the issues of cultural influence in chapter 12. However, all leaders possess the above two power resources to some degree.

This may sound obvious, but it is worth saying, because many Christian leaders either do not *feel* that they have power at their disposal or are easily blinded to the effects they can have on other people. Thinking of ourselves as weak servants we can draw the incorrect conclusion that we are powerless when we are not, perhaps especially if we feel overwhelmed by other powerful people in the church. It is common for us to have an unrealistic perception of the power dynamics and differentials that come with our role, but being careless to the issue raises obvious problems. Leaders who think they have no power find it hard to imagine they could be in danger of abusing power. Indeed, leaders commonly feel that where imbalances exist, they are on the disempowered end of them, for a wide range of reasons. It is common to find leaders struggling with imposter syndrome, brought about by an unsustainable set of expectations placed upon them, combined with a high level of public visibility and scrutiny. In such circumstances leaders might try to increase their authority for the sake of psychological self-protection.

It is no good pretending that as Christian leaders we have little or no power. We do. Power and power differentials are givens in leadership. Being realistic about this is essential if we are to grasp how we affect others. We need to be as insightful as possible if we want to ensure that we use our power and authority in right and godly ways.

Authority, used correctly, is a deeply positive, nurturing thing. We saw in the previous chapter that the goal of Christian leadership is to nourish the flock so that believers delight in the Lord and he is glorified in their lives. It is all about helping others grow in their relationship with Jesus, the Chief Shepherd, becoming mature in their own right. Healthy exercise of authority frees people to grow in maturity and service of God by instructing and equipping, providing structure, vision and direction. And, where necessary, correcting and occasionally disciplining.

The key principle, however, is this: power must be exercised wholly for the benefit of others and not for the benefit of the leader. Christian leadership, modelled on Jesus' leadership, is self-giving, not self-serving. As in the quote from 1 Samuel at the start of the chapter, the point is to strengthen others in God, not for them to serve the leader and the leader's purposes.

Suspicion of authority

Issues of authority and power are under intense scrutiny in society at large, and in churches. There is a high degree of sensitivity to issues of power imbalance, oppression and abuse, and rightly so. As Christians, we should be the first to recognize that we are all sinners and have the potential to go wrong in these ways, and we should also be the most committed to truth, righteousness and justice. The apostle John insists that living by the truth means walking in the light – in plain sight – and testing every spirit with discernment (1 John 1:3–7; 4:1).

However, it is possible to go beyond realism and into cynicism. It seems as though a widespread suspicion has taken hold that all authority and power is, at least in principle, inherently coercive, perhaps most of all when exercised by religious leaders. Underlying is the perception that leaders are only in it for themselves and not for the good of those they lead.

22

Positively, such sensitivity to authority makes it easier to hear and comfort victims of power abuse, expose wickedness, seek justice and insist on the highest possible standards among leaders. Negatively, it becomes easier to accept allegations of misuse of power as true and the accused as guilty until proved otherwise. Careful investigation may involve questioning people who are hurting, which can attract the additional charge of not believing victims. If due process might be interpreted as refusal to believe victims (or even worse, further violence against them), it becomes very easy to assume guilt and very difficult to prove innocence when an allegation is made. It is important to be aware that the power imbalance in churches is often strongly in favour of leaders rather than claimants. It is often very costly and difficult to bring accusations against people in positions of authority. But assuming that leaders are guilty before due process can mean that fair investigation becomes impossible, with any appeals of innocence viewed as further power plays.

The limits of elder authority[2]

In such a context, transparency and accountability regarding the exercise of authority become, if it were possible, even more vital.

Where the boundaries lie of appropriate, legitimate, biblical leadership authority tends to be unacceptably vague in most churches. If leadership authority is to be exercised healthily in the light, this needs to be clear. Different churches and denominations have different formal ways of expressing and defining the role that leaders play, how they are vested with authority, and where the limits of that authority lie. These may be explicitly drawn from Scripture or be the codification of historical practice. There are four main approaches:

---

2 I'm particularly grateful in this section for insights from Paul Coulter.

- Leaders may only mandate what Scripture commands.[3]
- Leaders may only mandate what the congregation has agreed.
- Leaders may only mandate what the denomination has agreed.
- Leaders may only mandate what the authority figure (supervisor/bishop/apostle) has taught.

Among the most common biblical descriptions of the job of elder are:

- Teaching – faithfully passing on the good news of Jesus, so that people receive the Word of God.
- Shepherding/overseeing, so that people become imitators of Jesus, and of leaders in as much as they are faithfully following Jesus.

Jonathan Lamb says:

> Leaders must therefore be people who are themselves submitted to that powerful word, whose lives are being shaped by its teaching, and whose ministry is enlivened and empowered by its dynamic effects. Leadership teams of all kinds need to ensure that the Bible is at the centre. It should be the controlling principle of church life and the daily sustenance of its leaders.[4]

My own view is that leaders' authority to mandate the belief and practice of individual believers is strictly limited to what is commanded in Scripture. All real spiritual authority derives from God via his Word. There is no right to impose anything beyond that on the conscience of other people, regardless of how noble the aim or how important the project. This does not mean that leaders cannot

---

3 I recognize that different traditions hold different views on who decides the acceptable bounds of interpretation of Scripture.
4 Harold Rowdon (ed.), *Church Leaders Handbook* (Partnership, 2002), 21.

appeal for other things on the basis of wisdom, knowledge, experience and shared goals. Nor that they cannot be delegated to carry out practical policies and arrangements of the church in agreed ways. But they cannot *command and insist* on beliefs and behaviours on the basis of their own personal authority. This is only legitimate on the basis of direct biblical teaching.[5]

There is a clear difference between leadership that is gentle and loving in its strength, and leadership that is forceful and overbearing. Shepherds lead others to walk in the ways of the Lord. Their authority is not that of lording it over people like a general (Mark 10:42), but of sacrificing themselves for others like a gentle, loving parent (1 Thessalonians 2); caring, guiding and protecting (Acts 20:28).

Leaders don't commend themselves by overriding the consciences of others, but through the plain, honest setting out of the truth, to which they too are subject. In short, leaders are not God. They are to point people to God and to what he has revealed in the Bible. They help people eagerly examine the Scriptures to see if what they are saying is true. As in Berea in Acts 17, they don't just insist that people take what they say on trust: 'Now the Bereans were of more noble character than the Thessalonians, for they received the message with great eagerness and examined the Scriptures every day to see if what Paul said was true' (Acts 17:11); 'By setting forth the truth plainly we commend ourselves to every man's conscience in the sight of God' (2 Corinthians 4:2).

Leaders who are reluctant to engage with Scripture, or who insist that their way is the only scriptural way without discussion ('I am the one trained in Scripture, and you have no right to question my handling of it'), or who demand obedience without reference to Scripture, are almost certainly outside the limits of legitimate authority. A key principle from the Reformation onwards has

---

5 Of course, this doesn't mean churches are obliged to associate with those who don't believe the same things or share the same vision of what they are called to do, simply because there is no explicit biblical command.

been that 'Scripture alone' has spiritual authority. The authority of leaders is only valid in as much as it plainly derives from Scripture. Leaders must be open to correction by the Bible.

We will explore many indicators that a leader may be exceeding the limits of healthy, biblical authority in subsequent chapters. Some obvious initial signs include:

- actions, decisions or lifestyle that clearly contravene Scripture;
- lording it over others – overriding people's conscience with leader control, rather than commending the Scriptures to them;
- demanding personal obedience, privately browbeating or publicly humiliating others;
- urging the church into beliefs or practices without reference to Scripture, or avoiding or obscuring inconvenient Bible passages;
- adding burdens, demands and expectations that Scripture does not;
- imposing leader authority outside of the boundaries of church life. This is sometimes done by reducing the whole of life to the missional community, thereby extending their own authority into every area, overriding personal liberty.

Power imbalance and pastoral practice

As we shall see, a key area in which misuse of power and position can subtly start to take hold is our practice of pastoral counsel or mentoring, especially one on one. This is where informal authority is most powerfully at play and the most obvious example of where leaders exercise relational power that is legitimate but not transparent, plural or easily accounted for. Power imbalance is inevitable here. Even if the leader doesn't perceive it, the recipient may. And even if neither does, it is still present.

Wise leaders know that honesty and self-awareness are vital in pastoral practice. The combination of experience, advice, personality, credibility, trustworthiness, gifting and personal investment means people are highly susceptible to taking what leaders say on trust. The possibilities for subtle manipulation are obvious. Mark Sterling from the Chalmers Institute says that if we are to avoid the dangers of pastoral relationships becoming coercive,

> People need to be free to make their own bad decisions rather than my good decisions. While I might be right, I can influence you to make a decision against conscience. And I might be wrong. And you just doing what I think is right doesn't lead to your growth in maturity.[6]

The point of servant leadership is the flourishing of others in their walk with God, but in a one-on-one (non-transparent, non-plural) relationship it is possible to tip from leading a person to grow in maturity in their own right to influencing them to do what we want.

In practice this highlights the need to distinguish between personally confidential details of specific pastoral relationships and publicly transparent processes, so that were any matter of potential abuse of authority to arise, the church may be assured both that confidentialities are respected *and* that proper scrutiny can be carried out by responsible and neutral people. For leaders this means that promises of confidentiality can never be completely inviolable and must never be used as an excuse to avoid legitimate oversight.

To give one example, suppose a church needs to sack an employee for underperformance, but wishes to do so generously and pastorally to avoid a stain on their record. It may well be right to withhold specific details from the church. It is never right to withhold details from church officers whom the church has a legitimate expectation will scrutinize the process. Not least because, in this example, there is a major power imbalance. To maintain both confidentiality and

---

6 In personal conversation.

27

trust in due process and the use of authority, the church should not know the details but must be confident that legitimate scrutineers do.

Occasionally churches and organizations use non-disclosure agreements (NDAs) as a way to legally enforce confidentiality. The use of NDAs has been widely and justifiably criticized. At the time of writing, the NDAfree campaign[7] is highlighting how these legal tools, originally developed to ensure confidentiality concerning sensitive business data, are being used instead for damage control by making matters such as redundancy payments and good references conditional on the silence of the weaker party.

I have yet to come across a situation where I think use of an NDA is legitimate and wise. They create an inevitable suspicion that they are deployed to protect the church or organization from reputational or financial damage, or legal challenge, serving the more powerful party at the expense of the weaker. It is next to impossible to avoid the impression that something shady has gone on, either that power has been misused in a calculated way to avoid legitimate scrutiny, or that bullying leaders have used hush money to legally enforce the silence of the powerless. People will – in fact, should – assume that something is amiss unless they have good reason not to. Where power imbalance is deliberately obscured from legitimate scrutiny, it is impossible to assure the church that all righteousness has been fulfilled for all parties. If the more powerful have no reason to be afraid because they are in the right, there is no reason to use an NDA to protect themselves.

NDAs are perhaps the most insidious example of 'accountability-capture' in a church or organization, where bodies that should hold leaders accountable are instead subverted to protect them, as I will discuss further in chapter 4. However, as the example of the church sacking the underperforming employee shows, the wider issue is how to make difficult decisions in the light of appropriate, legitimate

---

7   See: <www.ndafree.org/>.

scrutiny. In some denominations it is clear who appoints and oversees legitimate scrutineers; in independent churches it is often far from obvious. The danger is that those who exercise scrutiny are themselves captive to the interests and perspectives of those being scrutinized. In the worst such cases it has been possible for people to be removed from Christian leadership for abusive behaviour, but for the reasons to be kept quiet, allowing them to continue their behaviour in the wider Christian community.

Where there is any suspicion of accountability-capture, the effect on the credibility of leaders and due process, as well as trust in authority being used in a healthy and godly way, can be devastating. It is never enough for leaders alone to know that they have used their authority in a healthy fashion. Leadership authority is a public function. As such, everyone else needs to have confidence that it is being exercised in a healthy way.

I believe many churches and organizations are starting to wake up to the reality that without access to external and objective critical friends who can help with such process, it is much harder to maintain the objectivity that underpins organizational trustworthiness and healthiness. Churches are very wise to think carefully about both internal and external means of accountability.

Church discipline

Shepherding sometimes rightly involves more difficult elements of correcting and even rebuking: 'All Scripture is God-breathed and is useful for teaching, rebuking, correcting and training in righteousness, so that the man of God may be thoroughly equipped for every good work' (2 Timothy 3:16); 'These, then, are the things you should teach. Encourage and rebuke with all authority' (Titus 2:15). It is the job of leaders to protect the flock from false teaching, immorality and other sins that disrupt the church and bring shame and disrepute on its witness. These things should be rebuked with scriptural authority. However unpopular it may be, it is critical for the life and health of the flock to be clear what the Bible teaches to be wrong. For leaders to do nothing sends the message that sin is OK.

In our current culture, it is likely that right and godly church discipline will be labelled as hostile or abusive. One church leader told me about a situation where it was necessary to have a gentle cautionary word with someone, and it was met with the instant response: 'You [a man] are making me [a woman] feel unsafe.' The caution, which was meant in an entirely loving and positive way, was immediately countered by raising a safeguarding concern, with the additional suggestion of misogyny.

Claiming misuse of power can be a potent way to try to get leaders to back down and stop challenging wrong behaviour or teaching. However, if leaders do back down they abdicate their responsibility rather than healthily exercise their authority to pro- tect the flock. Here, Christian and secular views about how to love people diverge. Where secular culture believes a person's ultimate good is found in individual freedom, expression and self-defined identity, Christians believe it is found in knowing, loving and obeying Jesus. The respective views about what constitutes loving action towards them differ sharply, therefore, with Christians believing that it consists of encouraging them towards Jesus. Re- fraining from correction when someone is acting in ways that damage their love and commitment to him is a failure to love both them and the wider church.

In Matthew 18, Jesus provides a procedure for dealing with sin among Christians that is relational, incremental and proportionate:

> If your brother sins against you, go and show him his fault, just between the two of you. If he listens to you, you have won your brother over. But if he will not listen, take one or two others along, so that 'every matter may be established by the testimony of two or three witnesses.' If he refuses to listen to them, tell it

to the church; and if he refuses to listen even to the church,
treat him as you would a pagan or a tax collector.
(Matthew 18:15–17)

The process begins with private and prayerful pleading, and showing the person his or her sin. If this is rejected it becomes appropriate
to make it more public, first with a small number and then with the
church, ensuring accountability and transparency both for the individual and for those urging the person to repent. If this is rejected,
the final sanction is removal, but always with the loving aim of
repentance and restoration, not as vindictive punishment.

The New Testament has many examples of where church discipline
was necessary and discernment about proportionality was vital. In
2 Thessalonians 3:14–15 we read about dissociating from someone
who disobeys apostolic teaching, while still warning the person as a
brother or sister. However, 1 Corinthians 5 is much more serious
about excommunicating a blatantly sexually immoral person. There
is no hint of such an individual being considered a brother or
sister, though it's important to note that Paul's ultimate hope is that
the person being disciplined may be saved on the day of the Lord
(verse 5). In Revelation 2:20–24 Jesus himself could not be clearer
about not tolerating the false teacher 'Jezebel' who was leading the
church astray. There is no exhaustive list, but there are plenty of other
examples of teaching and behaviour that, unchecked, cause division,
lead disciples away from Jesus, destroy churches and bring shame
on the name of Christ.

Hebrews 12 reminds us that God disciplines us for our good, that
we might share in his holiness, but that no discipline is pleasant at
the time. The call to repent of our sins and turn to God for forgiveness and salvation sounds intolerant and unaffirming to the world.
In situations where church discipline is necessary, it is crucial to
distinguish between loving correction that may cause distress,
and hatefulness; between the discomfort that comes from being

31

challenged, and harm. Of course, this is in no way a justification for cruel or blundering leaders to bully people while claiming that they are merely exercising tough love. 'I'm only "speaking the truth in love"' (Ephesians 4:15) has certainly been weaponized by those who like speaking truth (or who claim they are) but are not very loving.

Leaders given the unenviable task of enacting church discipline can all but guarantee they will attract strong criticism, regardless of how carefully and lovingly it is done. Therefore, it is critical to exercise it with due process, governed by the criteria discussed in the previous chapter (accountability, plurality, transparency and embodiment in the church community), so it is clear that everything has been done carefully, lovingly and proportionately.

Finally, a church that handles discipline carefully and well is more likely to be able to respond appropriately when the person in need of rebuke and correction is a leader. Church discipline must apply without favouritism, to leaders just as much as to everyone else. The church that shies away from the healthy exercise of authority in the matter of discipline may discover it is less able and likely to hold leaders to account when necessary. Used properly, church discipline is a safeguard against abuse and other sins by leaders; misused, it can become subverted into a defence mechanism to protect leaders against dissent by silencing or removing whistle-blowers.

In conclusion, Christian leaders rightly have authority and power. It is impossible for them not to hold these. However, they are not unlimited, but rather carefully defined and constrained for the good of others. The issue is not whether power exists, but whether it is being exercised in a godly, servant way to nourish, feed, lead and equip the people of God.

Part 2

THE SLIPPERY SLOPE

3

Introducing the slippery slope

> Keep watch over yourselves and all the flock of which the Holy
> Spirit has made you overseers. Be shepherds of the church of
> God, which he bought with his own blood. I know that after I
> leave, savage wolves will come in among you and will not spare
> the flock. Even from your own number men will arise and
> distort the truth in order to draw away disciples after them. So
> be on your guard!
> (Acts 20:28–31a)

The most disturbing thing about Paul's speech to the Ephesian elders
at Miletus in Acts 20 is the prediction that not all of them would
remain godly leaders. People appointed as shepherds tend not to have
the intention of becoming wolves, yet some distort the truth in
plausible-sounding ways to manipulate disciples and draw them
away.

Sometimes wolves prey on the flock from outside with ravening
assaults and persecutions. Sometimes they come clothed as sheep.
But if wolves in sheep's clothing are dangerous, wolves in shepherd's
clothing are worse. And wolves in shepherd's clothing who insist that
loyalty to the gospel means personal loyalty to them are incredibly
dangerous. Perhaps the most fearsome predators of all are wolves in
shepherd's clothing who demand personal loyalty and manipulate
people by playing the 'wounded victim' card to cultivate sympathy
and compassion and to avoid critique.

I think few people actively set out to become a wolf or a Matthew
6-type hypocrite (although I have unfortunately met one or two).
Nevertheless, some who set out to be servants morph at some point

into wolves. Where do they go wrong and how does it happen? Is it possible to take the first steps into misuse of position and power completely unawares?

The spectrum

I find it helpful to think of the slippery slope as a five-stage spectrum of leadership beliefs and practices that moves from legitimate use of authority, through illegitimate use, and eventually to the most serious abuses. In this chapter I will introduce each category briefly and then explore them more fully in subsequent chapters. Figure 1 on page 37 shows the five distinguishable categories in the spectrum.

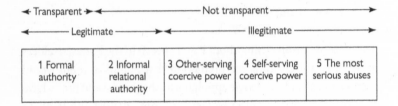

A. Legitimate and legitimated leadership
1 Formal, legitimate authority
2 Informal, relational legitimate authority

B. Illegitimate leadership
3 Illegitimate, other-serving authority
4 Illegitimate, self-serving authority
5 The most serious abuses

The boundaries between the stages are not precise and clear cut. While each stage has some obvious features, the thresholds are fuzzy and porous. It is easy to overstep them without realizing it, especially the boundary between Stage 2 (informal relational authority) and

Figure 1 **The spectrum, containing five distinguishable categories***

*The accompanying online resource is available at <https://ivpbooks.com/powerful-leaders>

Legitimated power; responsibly exercised in a godly way, formally with accountability and transparency	Legitimated power; responsibly exercised in a godly way, relationally by soft power and influence	Other-serving coercive power	Self-serving coercive power	The most serious abuses

Transparent ———— ►◄ ———— Not transparent

Legitimate ———— ►◄ ———— Illegitimate

Stage 3 (illegitimate other-serving authority). Moreover, leaders are more likely to move into the unhealthy, illegitimate categories when doing so would achieve some successful outcome with no obviously harmful consequences. People are less inclined to scrutinize means and methods when things are going well. More unscrupulous leaders understand well that the easiest point at which to increase their positional authority and power resources is when popular things are happening. Others do so unwittingly, but then discover that it is easier to move down the slippery slope than to crawl back up it. Reversing direction of travel might require confession of sin, perhaps even with threat to organizational position.

Once leaders discover that it is possible to act outside their formal authority and not be held to account for doing so, they have established that the paradigm in the church is amenable to it. Illegitimate leadership (Category B above) may still be sanctioned – or at least tolerated or have a blind eye turned towards it – because it has become an accepted part of the church culture, even though it shouldn't be.

Perhaps the biggest risk factor for leaders acting outside their legitimate authority is when churches have a sole minister who is expected to do everything. This risk increases even more in contexts with a high theology of priesthood or of anointing residing in that sole individual, or a strong emphasis on the singular vision of an entrepreneurial leader (for example, in some church planting cultures that wouldn't think in terms of priesthood or anointing). The whole set-up presumes they will exercise all the power. The church quite deliberately hands them all the authority. Congregations commonly find it hard to say what the limits on leaders' authority should be, and leaders are bad at self-limiting in the face of what can seem like unlimited demands and expectations placed upon them.

Perhaps we find it easy to sympathize with leaders who, in the face of unsustainable expectations, step outside their legitimate authority to 'get the job done'. But what happens in the process is that they discover they can exercise power that isn't rightfully theirs, and the church won't question it but rather allows them to act unaccountably. The unspoken understanding is that the minister is the CEO, so is probably authorized to do whatever they like. This is a first step towards people looking to the minister rather than to Jesus. However, now the ends can be used to justify the means. If leaders can bend, break or stand outside the rules for what seem like good reasons, there won't be anything to stop them from breaking the rules for bad reasons either. They have taken the first step out of the safety zone and may not even realize it.

Use and misuse of power and position: the Five Stages

Legitimate leadership

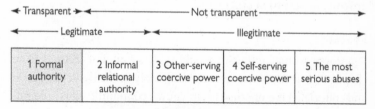

← Transparent →	← Not transparent →			
← Legitimate →		← Illegitimate →		
1 Formal authority	2 Informal relational authority	3 Other-serving coercive power	4 Self-serving coercive power	5 The most serious abuses

1 Formal, legitimate authority

Peter was the newly appointed pastor at Grace Church. Almost his first act as leader was to hold a meeting of the elders and deacons. 'The first thing I want to say to you is how critical it is to the church that this team is spiritually healthy,' he said, 'and I am no exception just because I am the pastor. In fact, I may be at greater risk, because the devil would love to tempt me and use me to damage the church. One area in which I want to be completely transparent with all of you and the church is how I use my position and power. I am the person in the church most at risk of misusing power, because I have more of it. I want to say in the hearing of everyone that if any of you think I am misusing my position in any way, you must help me. Come straight into my office – come together if necessary – and tell it to me straight. And I want to lead us to put in place policies and procedures that will ensure all our leading is done transparently, honestly and accountably.'

Peter is a leader whose self-awareness is likely to promote spiritual healthiness.

What type of power is involved at Stage 1?

It is legitimated use of authority, conferred, validated and overseen by an accountable legitimating body, for the carrying out of assigned responsibilities.

For whose benefit is power exercised?

Power is exercised clearly and transparently in service of the spiritual growth and health of others.

Features

Legitimate formal authority should evidence all four features from chapter 2. It is transparent, exercised visibly in the light; it is plural and collegial; it is embodied in the church community. It is accountable to agreed policies, procedures, protocols and best practice guidelines, the purpose of which are the good and the safety of all.

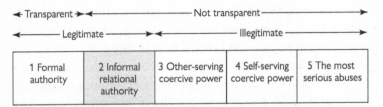

◄ Transparent ►	◄──────── Not transparent ──────────►			
◄──── Legitimate ────►	◄──────── Illegitimate ──────────►			
1 Formal authority	2 Informal relational authority	3 Other-serving coercive power	4 Self-serving coercive power	5 The most serious abuses

2 Informal, relational legitimate authority

Jane is a pastoral worker at St Sebastian's, where she is deeply appreciated for her sensitive manner and listening ear. People seek out Jane,
more than anyone else, for advice and encouragement.

One day Jane approached her vicar for advice. 'I love taking other
people under my wing and helping them grow, but I'm getting worried
that some of them trust me so much they will do what I say without
even thinking about it. It feels good to have people listen to me, but
I'm worried I could manipulate them without even knowing I was
doing it. How do I make sure this doesn't become unhealthy? Can you
help me think through the power I have in these situations and what
I need to do to make sure people don't become dependent on me?'

Jane's insight and humility will help her build collegial safeguards into her work that ensure discipling relationships avoid
co-dependency and unhealthy use of her relational power.

What type of power is involved at Stage 2?

It is legitimated use of responsible, relational authority.

For whose benefit is power exercised?

It is exercised for the good of others.

Features

This informal exercise of authority is not only normally entirely legitimate, but also relationally essential to the functioning of any church.
It is *highly* embodied in the community through the provision of
pastoral care, mentoring and discipling. If scrutinized it will normally
be seen to be entirely godly and responsible. However, the high degree
of embodiment commonly comes at the expense of reduced collegiality (it frequently happens relationally, one to one), transparency (it
often contains a degree of confidentiality) and accountability (it is
hard to ascertain the effect of relational influence, trust or popularity
built up between individuals, even for those involved, or to evaluate
the possible power discrepancies that can arise).

How do we get to this point?

We get here through features of relational ministry that diminish transparency, plurality and accountability.

Illegitimate leadership

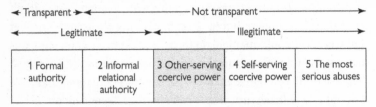

1 Formal authority	2 Informal relational authority	3 Other-serving coercive power	4 Self-serving coercive power	5 The most serious abuses

3 Illegitimate other-serving authority

Simon is an overstretched vicar of five small parishes. Not only is he expected to do everything in all the churches, he is regularly criticized for not doing it exactly the way wanted by all the different Parochial Church Councils (PCCs), which are jointly responsible with him for the running of each parish. He does have some sympathetic supporters in the congregations with whom he can be honest, however, and when two new families join one of the churches, he realizes there may be an opportunity.

Simon decides to pursue some changes that he knows will be opposed by the PCCs. However, if he can just persuade enough people in the congregations to support him, he can probably present his plans as a fait accompli and change the balance of power without including the PCCs. 'And where is the harm?' he reasons. 'The churches are in decline and will die unless I take this by the scruff of the neck. I can turn it around and bring new life, growth and direction, as long as I have conversations with supporters behind the scenes. I just need to avoid the PCCs getting wind of what I want to do until I have enough backing.'

Simon's motivation is entirely positive, but he believes he can only achieve what needs to be done by concealment and evading the authorized structures in the churches. It cannot be accomplished by authorized means, so he will need to do it some other way. He is in great danger of deciding that the end justifies the means.

What type of power is involved at Stage 3?

It is power that exceeds biblical boundaries and probably the original mandate conferred by the legitimating, overseeing body. Note, however, that it may still be sanctioned by that body, because nobody has yet spotted that anything is wrong.

This power exceeds appropriate relational boundaries, including becoming manipulative.

For whose benefit is power exercised?

Power is exercised in the belief that it is being used to serve others or the aims of the church. It is not self-consciously self-promoting.

Features

While there is probably no intention to abuse position and power, in reality there is evasion, avoidance or minimization of the checks and balances that accompany formal, legitimated, delegated authority. It is still highly embodied in the community and possibly collegial, but with reduced transparency and accountability. Leadership practice might still be sanctioned, but it ceases to be governed by agreed criteria and principles, and therefore can easily become manipulative and political. Leaders make themselves indispensable, gathering power and control to themselves, justifying what they are doing because it is done for the good of others. Lack of intention to harm does not mean that leaders have not strayed into sin. Believing that the ends justify the means, or illegitimately acquiring power, is sinful because you cannot lead for Jesus without leading in Jesus' way.

At the same time as minimizing checks and balances, leaders can use their increasing social capital to behave inappropriately in their pastoral relationships. A warning sign is when a leader is less concerned about truth or about being transparent than they are about achieving the desired outcome.

How do we get to this point?

We get here by using relational, soft power and influence to try to increase formal, organisational authority.

Relational influence is used as pressure to get people to achieve the leader's goals.

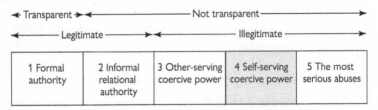

4 Illegitimate self-serving authority

Alex was a very popular assistant minister. There was just one problem: his boss Sam didn't like his popularity, and Sam's wife Sally struggled with insecurity. This came to a head one Sunday after Alex led a particularly good meeting. 'There you are, Sam,' laughed one church member. 'You've just done yourself out of a job!' Sam and Sally knew it was a joke, but it stung. Thereafter Sally was determined to find a way to get rid of Alex, and Sam felt there would be pressure at home if he didn't agree. He started to have private, unminuted discussions with individual elders about the concerns and disappointments he had with Alex not being a great team player.

Sometime later a parent made an offhand comment to Sally about their child not liking all the Bible studies in the youth group led by Alex. Sally took the opportunity to stoke more general discontent, and the writing was on the wall for Alex. Sam had raised enough concerns and minor niggles with the elders that this new complaint fitted well with the narrative he had constructed. When he told them that after much prayer he had decided the working relationship was no longer tenable, and it was either Alex or him, the elders were already predisposed to back him, or at least were unprepared to lose him. Alex was let go without a transparent process, and all queries from church members were met with vague replies that his performance had been lacking, but that it would be better for Alex if details remained confidential.

Sam has used his organizational position and a variety of manipulative strategies not to serve the church but himself, and has removed a perceived rival. It is very difficult to scrutinize what has actually happened, because the chief driver is Sally, whose role is invisible. In any case, Sam has sufficiently manipulated the elders who have scrutinizing responsibility in order to capture the mechanisms of accountability. Having got away with it, there is no reason not to act in this way again.

What type of power is involved at Stage 4?

It is power that intentionally and knowingly exceeds, evades, circumvents or captures the authority conferred by the legitimating overseeing body.

For whose benefit is power exercised?

It can no longer be honestly claimed that power is being used to serve others. It is exercised for personal advancement or self-protection.

Features

In Stage 4 more active coercion and control are evident. Leadership may still have features of embodiment in the community, but other people are now used as tools. They are discarded (or worse) when they cease to be useful or become a threat. Transparency is replaced first with privacy (perhaps under the guise of confidentiality) and then secrecy. Collegiality morphs into mutually protecting inner circles of yes-people, and accountability is intentionally avoided. Where other-serving illegitimate leadership tends towards manipulation, self-serving tends towards domination. A wide spectrum of self-defensive behaviours is in evidence, ranging from more subtle means of control to aggressive bullying.

How do we get to this point?

We get here when leaders use a combination of relational influence, increased personal power and reduction of organizational transparency, plurality and accountability to serve themselves.

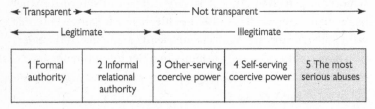

1 Formal authority	2 Informal relational authority	3 Other-serving coercive power	4 Self-serving coercive power	5 The most serious abuses

5 The most serious abuses of power and position

David was appointed and paid by his church to work in poverty-relief projects with a group of local churches and the council. He was given a church flat to live in. Everything was going well until he found out about an inappropriate relationship between an elder and a married woman in the congregation. David took the matter confidentially to his minister, who decided that it was impossible to raise the matter with the two people concerned without wrecking a marriage and 'leaving the church a smoking ruin'. He asked David to keep it as a matter for personal prayer, and the affair ceased after a period.

A year later the elder tried to arrange for his ex-lover to become church treasurer, at which point David spoke to the minister again. He was angrily told that he was raking up ancient history and potentially slandering two valued church members. He decided to blow the whistle and wrote to the regional minister, who replied that it was a local matter and he would not get involved. In the process, the regional minister copied the minister into an email to David, and the minister flew into a rage: 'You are criticizing my pastoral practice and integrity, challenging the reputation of an elder, trying to prevent the only qualified person becoming church treasurer, and you have to stop. If you don't withdraw your complaint and show some loyalty, there is no way the church will be able to continue to pay you or provide the flat. Now, will you or won't you?'

The minister has brushed the sinful behaviour of others under the carpet. The aggressive demand for loyalty is backed up by threats to David's ministry, livelihood and home. The regional minister's refusal to get involved means there are neither internal nor external mechanisms for accountability or whistle-blowing. The minister, elder and potential treasurer have to ensure David does not speak to others for the sake of their own reputations. David feels completely trapped. The bullying is very likely to succeed.

What type of power is involved at Stage 5?

It is aggressive domination, exploitation, control, threats and harm.

For whose benefit is power exercised?

It is exercised for the abuser's benefit, at the expense of others.

Features

None of the four features that characterize legitimate use of authority are present. Transparency is replaced with deliberate concealment and secrecy. There is no meaningful collegiality with anyone who is able or likely to challenge the abusive behaviour. Embodiment in the community is replaced with the creation and abuse of power imbalances. Accountability is premeditatively captured or corrupted in such a way as to deliberately legitimize, conceal and cover up abusive patterns, behaviours and paradigms. Opponents are intimidated, silenced, removed and gaslighted.[1]

---

1 'Gaslighting' is a specific type of manipulation in which the manipulator (usually with greater power resources) tries persistently to get another person to question their memory or perceptions. The aim is to undermine them by making them doubt themselves. Gaslighting should be carefully distinguished from due process of investigation, debate or mere disagreement.

Criminality may or may not be involved. But even when there is consent (for example, in the case of illicit relations between a minister and a congregant, which is neither criminal nor necessarily disapproved of by wider society), there is nevertheless both immorality and deliberate misuse of leadership power and position. Issues of genuine consent are also likely to be complicated and compromised by the power imbalances between leaders and those under them.

How do we get to this point?

We get here when personal power, advancement, control, dependency, insecurity and self-protection become defining features of a leader's sense of identity or position.

Slice by slice

The journey of a thousand miles begins with a single step. Leaders take the first wrong steps while still believing themselves to be servants motivated exclusively by helping others grow as Christians. Sin can work on different parts of our personality and motivations – our pride, ego, selfishness, self-deception, self-reliance or dependencies[2] – in remarkably subtle ways. The boundaries between the Five Stages are both blurry and porous because we are not objectively self-aware of the sinfulness of our hearts. They are easy to cross by drift and lack of care before leaders or anyone else notices but, once crossed, the new category easily becomes the governing paradigm for leadership behaviour and patterns.

How and why might leaders be tempted to extend their power illegitimately? In Matthew 6 it is to please others. Jesus condemns hypocrites who put on religious performances to manipulate applause and reward from people. Affirmation and acclaim are

---

2 From the Arrow Leadership Programme: *Overcoming the Dark Side of Leadership* (CPAS).

intoxicating. People like putting leaders on pedestals, and leaders can enjoy being there.

However, the driver Jesus highlights at the end of the chapter is worry and anxiety. There are particular pressures that result from Christian leaders having very few (actually, zero!) reliable metrics for success. They feel that people expect and demand success, and so establish wrong measures. How big is the congregation? How valued are their ministries? Are they being praised, or at least not criticized? Can they demonstrate that they are worth their pay by running programmes or creating new initiatives? When leaders lose their sense of confidence and security in God and his righteousness given to us, they easily find themselves driven by fear- or success-based understanding of what leaders should do. Most Christian leaders find that anxiety is a driver for their leadership practice at some point in their ministry. Maybe that was the trajectory that led the hypocrites in Matthew 6 into their ostentatious and performative giving, fasting and praying. The people loved it, but Jesus looked at the heart and identified it as nothing less than fake godliness manifesting itself through religious virtue-signalling.

4

From formal to informal power

[The] rulers of the Gentiles lord it over them, and their high officials exercise authority over them. Not so with you. Instead, whoever wants to become great among you must be your servant, and whoever wants to be first must be slave of all. (Mark 10:42b–44)

Messy Church was right up Mary's street and she loved being part of a recent church plant where she could give herself wholly to helping the church grow in such a warm, friendly and community-focused way. The church grew encouragingly from small beginnings, mostly because of key people like Mary, with strong relationships between them.

When they were nearing fifty in number Mary asked Bob, who along with his wife and another couple had begun the plant, when he thought the church would need some more formal leadership team structure and meetings. 'I've been so busy, I guess I've not really thought much about it,' Bob replied. 'And anyway, I'm not sure we need them. The relationships between the leaders are so healthy we'd rather rely on that than on rules to deal with things if there is a problem. We are all good people – trust us.'

Bob may struggle to move the church he has started into a healthy next chapter, because the relational authority significantly outweighs transparent accountable authority.

In this chapter we will look at the two legitimate categories of leadership authority and use of power: formal legitimate authority and informal and relational (but nevertheless legitimate) authority. Both can be exercised in wholly godly ways. However, the boundary between them is important, because it represents the point at which leaders can move from transparent use of authority and power to non-transparency. It is also the first point where it becomes possible for them to act unilaterally rather than collegially. This is a common first step towards exceeding authority.

Formal, legitimate authority

Formal, legitimate authority works by agreed criteria and mechanisms which are meant to ensure that power is exercised entirely in the light. Power for carrying out agreed responsibilities is delegated by a legitimating body (for example, a local church via its trustees, or a denomination via denominational officials and codes). It is exercised according to clear, agreed principles, practices and protocols.

In some missionary and church-planting situations there may be limited legitimating structures at first. It might be as small as a group of supportive friends. Wider legitimation then happens retrospectively. But a healthy church plant or missionary enterprise will look to quickly put in place formal means of being held accountable. We should be very cautious of leaders who self-appoint, particularly when based solely on self-proclaimed calling or anointing.

Formal, legitimated leaders and teams are open and transparent to scrutiny. They exhibit the four characteristics of accountability, plurality, transparency and embodiment in the church community. They actively embrace checks and balances on their leadership. People who advance their self-proclaimed calling or anointing often do so to avoid or delegitimize accountability.

Legitimated power is easily held accountable to checks and balances. Leaders are not merely open to accountability, they actively seek it out. They know that their hearts are as deceitful and open to sinful manipulation as anyone else's, and that leadership responsibility brings greater temptation and worse consequences when it goes wrong. The more senior and influential leaders become, the greater the risks they face.

It is not that legitimated authority and power can never go wrong. 'Regulatory capture' is a phrase sometimes used to describe a relationship that has become too close between regulatory agencies and the industries they are supposed to regulate. As already discussed, the Christian equivalent can be 'accountability capture', where the only people who can hold a leader accountable have a close relationship with them or are dependent on the continuing success of leader and organization for their own reputation and livelihood. Tragically, at the time of writing, there are numerous examples of leaders and organizations failing to address abuse because powerful individuals and groups have subverted, corrupted or avoided legitimate structures of accountability.

However, as a rule, authority that is exercised in plain view is less open to being misused. Those who exercise power according to agreed principles are much better protected against both temptation and allegations. Where possible, it is wise to consider both close-up accountability within the local congregation or close networks and denominational structures who might be able to spot issues sooner, and more arm's-length 'critical friends' who share values and theological convictions but are not chosen for their close personal relationship. For denominational churches, the wider hierarchy might help provide this, but it can also be dysfunctional. For independent churches, this can be sought out on a voluntary basis, undergirded by agreed best-practice principles. Agencies such as Thirtyone:eight are available if things get really bad and outside investigation is needed, but ideally healthy churches establish lower-level mechanisms that kick in well before that kind of support becomes necessary.

Principles, policies and procedures

As with church planter Bob, Christian leaders often have a bias towards relationships over regulations. The temptation is to see formal rules and structures as legalistic constraints that cramp godly opportunity. Perhaps a more helpful image is of seatbelts, which don't stop you driving – even driving fast – but protect everyone, including you, in the event of a crash. There is a well-known phrase that it's easier to ask forgiveness than permission. However, while that ability to act decisively (and apologize if necessary) might be needed in limited urgent situations, it should never be a general principle for leading in a church. In that context it is a sure-fire way to destroy trust and team-working. Certainly, regulations can sometimes bloat until they destroy any sense of freedom, but at their best, principles, policies and procedures are ways of expressing shared commitments.

Our *principles* are our fundamental and foundational beliefs, including what we believe about God, what we consider the gospel to be, other core doctrinal truths we are committed to upholding, and our understanding of the nature of the church and how it fulfils its purpose. Our *policies* publicly clarify how we operate, in order to work in the light. They kindle trust and credibility. Our *procedures* and *codes of practice* help enshrine that confidence in collegially accountable best practice and conduct.

Together they work to build confidence which, in turn, provides a huge boost to trust in leaders. When leaders try to act without trust, however legitimately, they cut against the grain. They can only accomplish what they have the trust to carry out, without trespassing into the illegitimate leadership categories. It is a mistake to assume that because a leader is acting in a godly and responsible way, everyone else can see and have confidence that they are. (The flip side of this is that leaders can accomplish illegitimate things if they can gain enough trust and credibility. Just being trusted doesn't mean that what you are doing is right.)

Principles, policies, procedures and codes of practice represent mutual commitment to walking together in the light. They provide boundaries that help everyone stay honest and form frameworks for accountability and scrutiny. Well-designed policies protect relation-ships and promote their flourishing; they don't stifle them.

Informal, legitimate authority

Formal authority is not the only kind of legitimate authority at play in Christian leadership. It is often not even the most powerful kind. Informal power resources frequently outweigh formal authority in terms of influence, and rightly so. However useful, policies and procedures do not make a family or church, as these are all about relationships.

Relational influence is informal and happens outside of, or parallel to, the sphere of formal policy and procedure. Christian leaders are frequently good at building social capital. Ministry often attracts caring people. Pastors by nature tend to be personable and good at working relationally. Indeed, they have a strong interest in doing so, because the work depends on a high degree of trust.

Several potential problems are immediately obvious. While formal structures can build trust, so do informal relationships, often much more so. Power is exercised by both means, but the primary reservoir of trust and credibility usually resides in relationships, which is also where the power of personality becomes a significant feature.

Personality is not the only factor in interpersonal relationships between leaders and others in churches. There are many other power dynamics at play. Psychologist Diane Langberg lists physical, verbal, emotional, knowledge, skill and position power; we might add personality, expertise, credibility, perceived trustworthiness, popu-larity, likeableness, personal vulnerability and friendship. Langberg comments: 'words, knowledge, skill and position can all be used in concert to move or convince another human being who is vulnerable.[1]

---

1   Diane Langberg, *In Our Lives First: Meditations for Counsellors* (Jenkintown, PA: 2014), 112–113, quoted in Bob Burns, Tasha D. Chapman and Donald C. Guthrie, *The Politics of Ministry* (Illinois: IVP, 2019), 159.

Relational influence is incredibly powerful in any circumstance, but when one of the parties is a respected leader it is almost impossible for there not to be some power discrepancy involved, possibly a large one. However, there is no reason this cannot be handled in an entirely godly way, and there are many benefits. Nobody wants an unapproachable, relationally poor minister, or one who can't be trusted.

The dangers of relational authority

Relational power is still legitimated power. Churches authorize pastors to disciple and care for people in the church's name and under its delegated authority. However, the embodiment of leadership now takes on a greater weight of relational authority, while accountability, plurality and transparency are all reduced, or may not even be present at all. The power dynamic changes, and is less in the light. Much relational ministry is exercised in ways that, if it does come under scrutiny, are seen to be godly and legitimate. I am not suggesting that all pastoring has an inbuilt drift in the direction of coercion. However, it is harder to scrutinize.

When leaders do drift towards illegitimate use of power and position, it often starts with non-transparent use of relational authority. The line between healthy social influence and subtle inappropriate manipulation is by no means always clear. Strong personalities can make people do things almost without realizing it.

Moreover, we are wired to believe and trust people we find likeable, and find it harder to believe that those with attractive personalities may be manipulating us. A particularly devious example of this is what Chuck DeGroat describes as 'fauxnerability' – false vulnerability.[2] Fauxnerability is an emotionally intelligent strategy whereby a carefully calculated display of weakness and emotional messiness is designed to influence people to respect and like us,

---

2 Chuck DeGroat, *When Narcissism Comes to Church: Healing Your Community from Emotional and Spiritual Abuse* (InterVarsity Press, 2020), Kindle Edition, 78.

creating dependency. It is a form of carefully concealed narcissism and relational domination disguised as openness and meekness, and it is very hard to disagree with. Perhaps secretly agreeing with the world that weakness is foolishness, fauxnerability provides a way for leaders to be applauded by churches for *appearing* weak without actually having to *be* weak. Fauxnerability is strength disguised. Fauxnerable leaders may realize they are doing it, or it may have become so ingrained as to have become their natural, subconscious way of working.

Power is convertible

Simon Walker points out that power is a commodity that can be accumulated: 'The other thing that must be appreciated is that power is a commodity. It is something that is possessed. You can accumulate power . . . Power is an asset that, over time, can be bought.'[3]

A key point is that not only can power be bought and accumulated but, just as with any other commodity, it can also be *traded*. As with different currencies, different types of power can be converted. Soft, relational power can be used to acquire hard, formal authority. The more our informal power resources outweigh our formal, account-able authority, the greater the temptation can be to try to use them to override, evade or expand the formal authority that has been entrusted to us. This might take the form of lobbying those with whom we have influence outside of formal structures, or trying to manoeuvre supporters into positions of authority.

Stepping out of the safety zone

Both forms of legitimate power, formal and informal, are present in every church, often exercised entirely properly in wise and loving ways within the limits of appropriate authority. However, while formal power is not immune from misuse and relational power is

---

3 Simon P. Walker, *Leading Out of Who You Are: Discovering the Secret of Undefended Leadership* (Manchester: Piquant Editions, 2007), 37.

frequently not misused at all, the relational is less transparent and so needs to be governed and overseen by formal accountability if we are to have confidence that it is being exercised appropriately.

To summarize, the first, biggest and easiest step into abuse of leadership position commonly occurs when leaders use their informal power to try to increase their formal power, or otherwise to evade or avoid the legitimate constraints upon them. When they use their *ability* to act (= power) to increase their *right* to act (= authority) or to evade accountability, it shows they think it is more important for them to be empowered to lead than it is to be constrained by agreed principles and plural decision-making. At that point the door to manipulation is wide open.

5

From legitimate
to illegitimate power

Rather, we have renounced secret and shameful ways; we do
not use deception, nor do we distort the word of God. On the
contrary, by setting forth the truth plainly we commend
ourselves to every man's conscience in the sight of God.
(2 Corinthians 4:2)

Two things were clear to Henry: first, dragging the church services
into the twenty-first century meant introducing more contemporary
worship material, and second, one of the deacons, Susanna, had a
visceral dislike of anything modern and vetoed every attempt by
force of personality. The constitution, however, made it very difficult
to remove her.

When the church entered a very pressured phase, Henry seized
the opportunity to delegate a wide variety of functions to sub-groups,
to relieve the deacons. Having talked individually with the other
deacons beforehand, Henry obtained agreement that the sub-groups
would have authority to make decisions and changes in a deacons'
meeting from which he knew Susanna would be absent. The rest of
the deacons agreed, and none of them questioned the process.

Has Henry done anything wrong? After all, the great majority
support him and it may well not be a wrong step for the church.
However, the only way he could obtain his desired outcome was by
manipulation and by concealing what he was doing from someone
who, within the church structure, had a legitimate right to know. The
church and the deacons have just unwittingly entered a new phase

of leadership where illegitimate means won't be questioned as long as they get an outcome that pleases the majority.

In the last chapter we considered the interplay between formal and informal authority and power resources. The significant differences between them are the levels of accountability, plurality and transparency. I suggested that a common first step into the danger zone is when leaders knowingly or unknowingly use their informal, relational power to evade, override or extend their formal authority. In this chapter we will consider the next shift, which is from legitimate use of authority, position and power to illegitimate.

It is useful to distinguish illegitimate, *other*-serving power from *self*-serving power because the motivation is different. With other-serving, illegitimate power, we want to achieve great things for God and his church but act as though the ends justify the means. It is not intentionally ungodly, and leaders may have no thought of serving themselves, grabbing power or dominating. While the desires may be good, however, the method of achieving them is toxic, acting 'in the flesh', in human strength, rather than depending on God. It may look like kingdom work, perhaps, but is not done in kingdom ways.

Illegitimate leadership in both the other-serving and self-serving categories depends to a lesser or greater degree on manipulation. In neither category is leadership being exercised fully in the light or is accessible to legitimate oversight, checks and balances. While illegitimate leadership may still officially be sanctioned, leaders are nevertheless starting to get used to the unaccountable and subversive exercise of power.

Why is this so tempting?

Before we explore some of the features of other-serving, illegitimate power, we should consider a few reasons why leaders might be tempted down this sinful path. Perhaps we need look no further than

Yoda's summary in *The Empire Strikes Back*: the dark side is quicker, easier and more seductive.

1 Ambition

In an address to the Living Leadership Refresh Online Network, Mark Sterling said: 'If grace as a gift is not enough to make us content and secure, then nothing ever will be. Do we get that? If we don't, it is the root of leadership abuses.'[1] His point is that being secure in God means we don't need to be ambitious. He continued: 'Ambition means I have to become more, because I am insecure and do not already have what satisfies me. If we think we already have everything in Christ, we don't need to.'

Needing to obtain or to become more is in essence what Philippians 2:3 describes as selfish ambition or vain conceit. The apostle Paul says it is the opposite of Christ-like humility. However, it is easy to convince ourselves that we are pursuing success not for ourselves but for other people and the kingdom of God. Power is never the only dynamic in play, of course. There is also love, service, sacrifice, the desire for lost people to be saved, self-deception and sin in our hearts. Leaders can feel that the desire for more is driven by holy zeal and not by selfishness or neediness.

2 Inadequate power for our responsibilities

Many churches have a lone minister who is expected to do everything (or at least it feels that way). The church deliberately hands over all the authority and presumes the leader will exercise power. In some denominations this may be explicit in the constitution or even the theology of leadership. Additionally, churches want to see results, usually in terms of activities, programmes, numbers, or personal attention from the leader. All leaders have felt the pressure of people wanting them to be all things. When this happens, it is unsurprising

---

1 From an address to the Living Leadership Refresh Online Network, October 2020.

if they begin to believe they need to have increased power to serve other people or fulfil the mission of the church.

Church leaders have a wide and complex range of responsibilities. One church leadership team asked how many hours I thought their minister worked in a week. When I said around sixty-five to seventy hours they were horrified. They simply had no idea how long it takes to prepare a sermon, the extent of pastoral visitation, or the number and complexity of pastoral burdens. It is unusual for a congregation to have an accurate understanding of what a minister does or the weight of burdens carried for other people.

So it is understandable if ministers often feel that they have been given responsibilities without the necessary resources and permissions to carry them out. It is unsurprising when leaders seek to extend their authority and increase their power so that it is equal to the responsibilities. It is hard to solely blame an individual for exercising power in illegitimate ways when the expectations of their role essentially demand it; churches and cultures also share some responsibility.

3 Wanting to please people

When churches expect leaders to do all the ministry of the church for them, leadership becomes about providing religious services for consumers rather than equipping disciples for their own service and ministry. Churches affirm leaders in being a one-man band and resist when they try to change the expectations.

This is exacerbated when powerful people or groups express their disappointment or disapproval if leaders don't deliver what they want. In other instances, leaders can become beholden to others by friendship or agreement with the ideas of a group within the church, and then find they are the unfortunate choke-point between people with strong views (some of whom they may be relationally close to) and formal structures of authority and accountability with which they may or may not agree. If a powerful interest group encourages a leader to act in ways the leader agrees would be good for the gospel – for example, ditching choral music in favour of a youth-led band to reach a younger generation – but which cannot be done by legitimate means, it is still wrong for them to do it. Seemingly valid goals do not justify subversive means, even at the suggestion of friends.

4 Frustration with people

All leaders know the frustration of people not understanding or buying into their vision. The temptation is to try to change people by their own strength into their vision of what they should be. On one occasion I was asked to speak to a Christian Union houseparty before a large mission event. In the large public group, everybody was enthusiastic for the event. In private conversation almost nobody was. They were being pushed into it by leaders from local churches, who were motivating them not with grace but with guilt, the underlying implication being that failure to get on board with the project with the appropriate enthusiasm was unfaithfulness to God. The students all knew how to look good and say the right things in the large body, but their hearts weren't in it.

In fact, they had become tools for the vision of the church leaders, whose frustration to see the university evangelized to a greater degree created an unhealthy culture of pressure and fear. The subtlety was that it would be great to see more evangelism going on in the university. It was a good aim, but the way of going about achieving it was to get fearful people signed up to the cause by illegitimate means.

Features of illegitimate use of power

It's not hard to see the appeal of abusing leadership authority. As per the thoughts from Yoda above, those who do this find it easier and quicker to get results. Those who choose the godly way might seem ineffective by comparison. Right at the heart of the issue is the temptation to manipulate, to use one's ability to act to increase one's right to act. It can happen in a few different ways:

1 Leaders use their power manipulatively to gain control over formal structures, policies and procedures.
2 Leaders use their power to remove checks and balances on themselves, so even if they obtain no greater formal authority, nobody can meaningfully challenge them anyway.
3 Leaders use their power to gain control over enough people through relationships or unhealthy pressure.

That is, they convert soft power into hard power or they evade accountability, or a combination of the two. The distinction is worth making, because it means that subsequently they misuse power and position in three different ways:

1 By obtaining authority illicitly. They actually acquire the authority and can then use and abuse it.
2 They don't actually acquire the authority, but by ensuring they won't be challenged can act with impunity anyway.
3 By co-opting enough people to act as a majority or provide an alibi if they are challenged. This is similar to 2, but the reason the leader can act with impunity is because they have fooled gullible dupes. People who, if the leader is ever called to account, can say, 'Well, I never witnessed them behaving like that.'

To illustrate this with a financial example, in the first case they set things up so that they can sign off their own expenses without scrutiny. In the second case, someone else approves the expenses but the leader has persuaded the person to rubber stamp them. And in the third example they can claim whatever they want because enough people have been persuaded that they are honest and would never commit fraud.

In the first case, formal structures, systems and norms for accountability are actively taken over and corrupted, while in the latter two they are just ignored. The first is perhaps more malign because it is harder to correct, but in all three effective oversight and accountability are deliberately reduced. Initially this allows leaders to feel they are getting more done efficiently, with fewer hindrances. They are able to act unilaterally, believing the increased freedom is a tool to serving others. However, in reality they have started to use strength to control people. The integrity with which things are done is now impossible to assess.

Imagine the minister who has many other leaders in the church struck down by COVID. Over the space of eighteen months the minister gets used to making all the decisions, preparing all the virtual meetings, doing all the administration and writing all the cheques. As the country starts to move out of more severe lockdown, the minister is faced with groups that have wildly different agendas. One elder insists that the church should never have stopped meeting together to begin with. Another insists that to gather again too soon is tantamount to not loving your neighbour. Still another is caring for a close relative in a high-risk category and says there is no way they can continue to serve if the church starts physical meetings. The minister feels the only way to make sense of it all and bring unity is to require everyone to fall in line with their wisdom on the issues or no longer continue to serve in leadership. Everyone reluctantly agrees, because firm leadership is at least better than chaos.

As this becomes normal, the minister is in danger of creating a bubble. The only narratives given airtime are the ones that affirm the minister's views. Leaders are chosen or resign accordingly until eventually the whole leadership structure is organized solely around the minister, whose decisions are now law. There was no intention to be self-promoting at the start, but now the minister's leadership is (in their own eyes, at least) indispensable. They control all the ministries and ratify all decisions. Disagreement is received as destabilizing the church and the minister easily conflates the good of others and the need for stable leadership with getting their own way.

When leaders wholly control structures, organizational paradigms become indistinguishable from their vision, desires and ways of doing things. Systems shift subtly from protecting gospel integrity to protecting both the paradigm (tradition, tribe, methodology) and the leaders who embody it. This instils the belief that the leaders cannot be wrong, or at least cannot be challenged, and everything becomes impervious to critical examination even by authorized scrutineers (for example, church elders or denominational officials) until something catastrophic forces it. It is quite possible for leaders to become self-promoting without realizing it. Over time, defending their reputation becomes important to retaining and growing control. They become harder to disagree with because of the combination of the control they exert within the formal structure and the relational support they can gather privately outside of it. While others may not yet be disenfranchised or removed, disagreement nevertheless starts to be seen as disloyalty and can be loaded with consequences. It might be seen in:

- expressions of disappointment that others are not on board, presumably because they don't really understand, or lack wisdom;
- interpreting questioning as lack of commitment, faith or vision;
- receiving critique and correction as evidence that the questioner lacks the necessary maturity to contribute meaningfully;
- creating binary choices that demand others back down: 'If you want these outcomes you need to either back me to accomplish them or sack me'; 'It's either them or me'.

The slippery slope

The far terminus of this trajectory is still a long way off, but the church has started to become a shield for the protection of the leaders.

None of this happens all at once but by small steps, none of which on their own are problematic enough to suggest leaders might be in danger of becoming coercive. There is always an understandable justification, perhaps a lack of manpower requiring a leader to assume a greater degree of control, or a new opportunity to advance the mission in fresh and exciting ways. As already noted, the more apparently successful a leader is at delivering ministry aims, the more good outcomes can be leveraged to increase positional authority and power resources. This is even more the case when there are external threats to doctrinal orthodoxy and the leader can insist on personal loyalty in order to defend biblical truth.

However, when leaders use the combination of relational capital and personality power to exceed or redefine the limits of their legitimate authority, they create the toxic and unacceptable precedent that they may now act as they please and are beyond scrutiny. They may still justify their way of acting by their legitimate ends, but given the way sin corrupts, it is no surprise if this then spirals into serving, promoting or protecting themselves. And underneath there are always spiritual issues: the desire for power reveals an unbelief in Christ's power and goodness; the need for control reveals some deeper lack of trust in God.

6

From serving others to serving self

> But mark this: There will be terrible times in the last days. People will be lovers of themselves, lovers of money, boastful, proud, abusive, disobedient to their parents, ungrateful, unholy, without love, unforgiving, slanderous, without self-control, brutal, not lovers of the good, treacherous, rash, conceited, lovers of pleasure rather than lovers of God – having a form of godliness but denying its power. Have nothing to do with them.
>
> (2 Timothy 3:1–5)

Mark was a winsome and kind pastor. But he also liked power a bit too much. Little by little he started to offer himself to chair more and more teams and boards: 'I will happily take that on to free up other people from being too busy.' He did this slowly and carefully, but after five years there wasn't a single decision in the church that didn't have to get his approval. Nobody imagined there was a control agenda going on, simply because he was so nice.

In the process Mark managed to ensure that the majority of the posts on the salary committee were occupied by his friends. One day they sent someone for a quiet word with the treasurer, saying they thought Mark deserved what the treasurer thought was a disproportionately large pay rise to reflect his experience and seniority. The treasurer looked at the church constitution to find out how to express concerns about this, only to discover that it had been rewritten the previous year, making Mark the person through whom all concerns had to be addressed. He decided to approach him, but Mark insisted that it was inappropriate for him to be in a discussion in which he had a financial interest: 'I'm sure you can understand that I need to be at arm's length from any process or decisions undertaken by the salary committee.' There was literally nowhere else for the treasurer to take his concern.

There is at least the possibility that Mark has a strategy for accumulating control, consolidating power through manoeuvring his friends into influential positions, and removing accountability mechanisms. But if so, it is subtle and long-term and unlikely to be challenged if done carefully enough. Churches are wired to not imagine a trusted, pleasant pastor could be that intentionally manipulative. The thing to watch out for in this case would be what happens to the treasurer if he continues to express his concerns.

The frightening thing about the 2 Timothy passage at the start of the chapter is that wolves don't look like wolves, but have an appearance of godliness. They say the right things and project the right image, but are in it for themselves. Jude speaks of shepherds who feed themselves rather than the sheep (Jude 4).

Self-serving leaders begin coercing people into supporting them by being winsome. They are charming when everyone is acquiescent, only revealing their true colours when challenged. Being pleasant is part of the pathology of control. If self-serving leaders are to build themselves up and undermine other people, it is vital for them to make themselves as agreeable and believable as possible. A devastating comparison is given in 2 Corinthians 11:13–15:

> For such men are false apostles, deceitful workmen, masquerading as apostles of Christ. And no wonder, for Satan himself masquerades as an angel of light. It is not surprising, then, if his servants masquerade as servants of righteousness. Their end will be what their actions deserve.

The self-serving, self-promoting leader (or 'super-apostle' in this case) can be crafty and convincing, charming in every sense of the word.

As we move into the category of self-serving, illegitimate authority, it can no longer be honestly claimed that power is being used to serve others. It is being used to serve ourselves. However, as already noted, the thresholds are fuzzy, so it is just possible that leaders who cross the threshold into serving self may not understand that they are doing so. They hang on to the last vestiges of the idea that it is about others by entirely identifying the good of others and the success of the ministry with their own personal position.

The tactics of self-serving leaders become ever more actively coercive. If they are still embodied in the community, it is not in order to model Christ, but to put themselves in the centre and foreground. Transparency is replaced with secrecy. Plurality is now meaningless. If it even still exists, it has become an impenetrable and mutually reinforcing inner circle. Accountability is intentionally dismantled. There are now strong, if unspoken, disincentives to challenge leaders, and negative repercussions for those who do.

Why is this tempting?

In a few words: power, protection, advancement and safety. There is enjoyment to be found in the power of calling all the shots and creating a safe and impervious context in which to do so. The vicious circle is alluring: leaders use power to acquire additional authority, which in turn can be used to increase power resources still further. Good motives are fading. Now it is about self-promotion and self-protection.

All the way back to Genesis 3 we can trace twin instincts. On one hand the human heart has been hard-wired to seek solitary, authoritarian power and safety. On the other, there is a deep-seated responsibility-abdicating acquiescence to ungodly leaders or groups.

The slippery slope

All leaders are to some degree aware that there is an inbuilt inclination to want to be a free agent, holding positions of honour and power. Ruling over people with strength feeds a primal neediness. But in a church setting where power is meant to be in the process of being redeemed, the self-serving leader also needs to create a deceptive outward appearance of being a shepherd. When Jesus called down woes on the Pharisees, the presenting issue he focused on was their self-promotion at the expense of justice and the poor:

> Woe to you Pharisees, because you give God a tenth of your mint, rue and all other kinds of garden herbs, but you neglect justice and the love of God. You should have practised the latter without leaving the former undone. Woe to you Pharisees, because you love the most important seats in the synagogues and greetings in the market-places.
> (Luke 11:42–43)

It is also possible for leaders to become jealous. Seeing the promotions and worldly benefits that some of their peers in secular employment start to acquire, Christian leaders can believe they are owed some kind of church-related equivalent that reflects their seniority, including influence, acclaim, platforms, people willingly following their leadership, or at least being grateful and not criticizing all the time. This desire can get worse with age and length of service.

In his third letter, the apostle John warned his friend Gaius about a man called Diotrephes 'who loves to be first' (3 John 9). He tried to be top dog by gossiping maliciously about apostles, refusing to welcome genuine believers and putting those who did out of the church. Having got the power, he proceeded to use it to secure his position by disenfranchising any real disciples who might prove a challenge to his leadership, and apostles who might bring corrective teaching or rebuke. The first step after any successful power grab is always to remove the opposition.

All of this, says Jesus, reveals what is in leaders' hearts: 'Now then, you Pharisees clean the outside of the cup and dish, but inside you are full of greed and wickedness' (Luke 11:39). They looked good on the outside – it seemed that they could lead people closer to God – but it was a masquerade. They were exploiting religious respectability in order to oppress people through the use of religious power. Goggin and Strobel describe this virtue-signalling spin well, as 'shrewd self-engineering'.[1]

Self-protection

It doesn't always have to do with being top dog, however. Accumulation of power can be about leaders minimizing fear and protecting themselves from perceived threats and pressures. The pressures leaders face in no way excuse the misuse of power, but some understanding of the pressures can help us recognize when we or others might be in the danger zone.

The first factor is a broad, often unrealistic, range of expectations and responsibilities. Leaders have a wide range of complex responsibilities, some of which they are good at and some of which they aren't. They are expected to deliver these anyway by people who assume ministerial omnicompetence while having no idea of the extent of the burden. When three or four different kinds of complex issues, or several heavy pastoral burdens, coincide in the church, everyone struggles.

Second, leaders can experience emotionally debilitating imposter syndrome. They know they are meant to minister out of weakness and powerlessness (2 Corinthians 12), in which God's strength is manifested, but weakness and powerlessness can produce imposter syndrome. Leaders feel they have to smile at everyone, help and

---

1   Jamin Goggin and Kyle Strobel, *The Way of the Dragon or the Way of the Lamb: Searching for Jesus' Path of Power in a Church that Has Abandoned It* (Thomas Nelson, 2021), 37.

empathize with everyone, never gripe and absorb all criticism, being unfailingly positive and definitely never, ever sinning. All the while knowing inside it is a facade.

In effect leaders can feel obliged to lie, or at least to present a fantasy picture. They carefully bury all the problematic parts of themselves so that nobody ever sees them. Even when they are trying not to, other people project the fantasy picture on to them anyway. They find they cannot escape being the vessels for everyone else's hopes, fears, tragedies, criticisms and desires for what their church and their own Christian life could become. However, they lack the emotional or occupational safety nets that go with other caring professions. This is a critical area in which churches and leaders simply have to develop better structures for support than most have at present. I will say more about this in chapter 10.

These things are designed to drive leaders out of experiencing the love of God. Satan loves to stoke the inadequacy and fragility that causes them to receive contrary opinions as threats. Common coping strategies include denial, avoidance and unhealthy or sinful habits for self-soothing. A chief one is to become a control freak who gathers power. Some leaders attempt to mitigate fear factors and counter imposter syndrome by adducing credentials, carefully curating an image of being the Qualified One.

Exercising power, then, can be about indemnifying ourselves against frailty and perceived inadequacy. A significant initial step is when leaders first cover up some minor sin or error. If they choose to conceal rather than confess, when questioned about a dubious decision, a mistake or a small deceit, they will probably double down when the questions can't be deflected. They then become guilty not only of the original sin but also of hiding and excusing it to avoid responsibility and repentance. How important it is to get into the habit of bringing such things into the light quickly.

Features of self-serving power

When leaders get into the self-serving category they are fully immersed in the dark side of power. The more insecure they become, the more attractive it is.

The first feature of self-serving power to be aware of is the mechanisms by which control is consolidated. It can begin with a popular leader having a strong and recognized sense of personal vision for how to advance the mission of the church. But when this is seen as a calling from God, it can be hard to question the leader or vision without sounding as if you are opposing the will of God.

Churches and mission agencies are strongly vision- and values-led organizations that pray regularly for God-revealed insight. Moreover, like all vision-and-values organizations they can fall into the trap of wanting not just loyal participation from members and employees, but a sharing of heart, life and wholehearted, unquestioning agreement too. Missions are often entrepreneurial, and founders look for people to join them who share their passion and utter commitment.

Christians sharing passionate commitment, or a church having a strong sense of being on a mission together, can be good and healthy. It is often a very positive feature when churches expect a high degree of commitment from believers in their walk with the Lord. Close, committed communities do not inevitably head in an abusive direction.

However, strong communities amplify the possibility of both good and harm. The better something is in the first place, the worse it becomes in the hands of leaders exercising unaccountable and absolute authority. Good emphases can mutate into expectation of a high degree of submission to them. An oppressive assumption can take hold that obedience to them – and to the rest of the community that is committed to them – is how we live out our commitment to the Lord and the gospel. People are praised and brought to the foreground when they serve the leader's purposes. As Chuck DeGroat puts it, this is because they are really extensions of the leader's ego.[2] They become submissive partners in a toxic co-dependency in which they are fed by praise from the leader, and the leader is fed and protected by the obedience of the followers. Becoming a tool for the fulfilment of the leader's vision is almost a condition of membership.

This self-promotion can be reinforced with the belief that the organization owes the leader for sacrificial service, or by a culture where no-one else's views can be expressed because 'they don't understand Christian ministry'. It can even be directly presented as divine. In different settings, this could be expressed as:

- 'I've prayed extensively about this';
- 'I had a prophetic word';
- 'I am the priest (or preacher) between you and God';
- 'God has told me, and I have no doubt at all that this is what God is saying to the church'.

Each of these, when wielded in the cause of control, is not very subtle code for 'I'm in charge, so back off'.

Strategies for capture and control

Once the underlying narrative has been captured, the system is wide open to being corrupted. The leader and their supporters now have a variety of ways to control both structures and people. The aim is to set the terms of their power and position themselves, by wholly controlling the organization, creating dependency upon themselves and forcing acquiescence, or, when this is resisted, by bulldozing the opposition. Tactics can range from subtle to extremely aggressive.

---

2   Chuck DeGroat, *When Narcissism Comes to Church: Healing Your Community from Emotional and Spiritual Abuse* (InterVarsity Press, 2020), Kindle Edition, 79.

1 Capturing and controlling structures

Coercive leaders ideally want control over authority structures, especially structures of accountability. Where this is not possible, dismantling them is the preferred strategy. At the subtle end this can begin with creating dependency on themselves, either with people who allow them access to greater authority, or with those they can put in positions of influence and subsequently control. It is easier for an inner circle to control structures than it is for a single individual. More obviously domineering tactics can then come into play, including:

- controlling all boards, agendas and church programmes;
- privately arranging predetermined outcomes with close associates;
- nepotistically manipulating preferred candidates into leadership positions and removing unwanted ones;
- establishing executive groups that remove accountability or scrutiny from legitimate bodies such as trustees or elders, disempowering them and preventing them from fulfilling their oversight role;
- insisting on obedience to supposed God-given mandates;
- refusing evaluation of their work by others;
- using external authorities to silence, override or dismiss concerns raised in the local church.

All this is done in the service of intentionally gaining control of organizational governance and authority structures.

2 Controlling or bulldozing people

Here again there is a spectrum of tactics from subtle to aggressive. They can be deployed against both those who disagree with or stand up to leaders, and those dear to them.

More subtle tactics for marginalizing opposition can include:

- silencing others by denying they have the right, the necessary insight or experience to contribute;
- manipulation through easy apology, insincere praise, or suggestions that they have merely been misconstrued;
- passive aggression;
- faux-vulnerability;
- hyper-sensitivity in areas where leaders have made mistakes;
- refusing to admit sin and failure, apologize or repent (for fear of reputational damage).

More aggressive approaches are designed to actively diminish opposition through wounding, traumatizing or eliminating people. A useful acronym from the world of psychology and trauma studies is DARVO. The aggressor:

- **D**enies that anything is wrong;
- **A**ttacks the challenger;
- **R**everses **V**ictim and **O**ffender.

This is easily spotted in politics, where truthful challenges are dismissed as 'fake news'. But it is a feature of self-serving leaders in all spheres, including churches. It may be exercised by leaders empowering themselves through

- making themselves inaccessible except to the inner circle;
- evading standard processes and protocols, especially ones to do with accountability: annual reviews and negligence, grievance or conflict-of-interest policies;
- ensuring any evaluation or investigation of themselves is neither independent nor impartial;
- actively covering tracks, lying, deceit;

- identifying outside threats that can only be met by themselves. The worse the threat, the more power they may be permitted to consolidate;
- grooming both victims and those who can provide cover or alibis.

It might also be exercised by disempowering others:

- destabilizing those who might be a threat to the leaders' authority;
- isolating people so they can be more easily dominated, perhaps by discouraging or forbidding others to speak to them, using strategies that divide and conquer;
- ridiculing or silencing opposition;
- attacking credibility, labelling those who don't buy into the vision as lacking vision, faith, commitment or competence;
- expressing anger or disappointment in a way that puts people down and humiliates;
- blame-shifting: 'I'm so disappointed you would think that' (i.e. 'It's you, not me; you misunderstand the situation/me; you lack the necessary facts or judgement';
- implying the victim is the guilty party, with requests that they be the one to apologize: 'I'm so sad that the relationship with that person has broken down, but it's their fault, not mine.' Asking a victim for an apology places them in an impossible situation. If they apologize for anything, perhaps in the hope that it will be reciprocated and will improve the situation, the abuser doesn't reciprocate but simply uses it as evidence of their victim's guilt and their own innocence. But if they don't apologize, the abuser can say they went looking for reconciliation but were rebuffed. Heads I win, tails you lose;
- refusing access to communication channels for those who wish to express concerns to the church;

- ostracizing people who express concerns, or making life hard for their family and friends;
- gaslighting;
- casting doubt on people's character, emotional stability or sanity, thus stigmatizing them;
- utilizing non-disclosure agreements.

Some of these tactics work by controlling the organization, some by threats, and some by intimidation, attack, isolation or character assassination. Some combine the organizational and the personal, perhaps by getting the organization to distance itself from those who might challenge the leader, or by insisting other people distance themselves, or by bringing other social pressure to bear. Whistle-blowers know all too well that if they challenge coercive leaders it probably won't just be them who are ostracized, but their families also.[3]

Some work more simply by deferral and delay. Bad leaders know that if they ignore people and refuse to engage with them for long enough, they will probably give up and go away eventually. This is preferable to removing them or otherwise overtly causing them to leave, because it allows the leader to disclaim responsibility afterwards, placing it instead on those who have left and are now out of the picture. The real reasons for their departure can then be airbrushed out, their concerns removed from the record, or their reputation trashed.

The aim is to control structures, bully individuals who pose a threat, and neuter any concerns before they can be aired. As Mark Meynell puts it, 'these make it hard for someone to decline or disagree or even just ponder'.[4] We must see these things for what

---

3 The list is far from comprehensive, concentrating mainly on the areas of coercion and manipulation. I don't intend to minimize the severity of other fields of potential abuse, such as online grooming.
4 <www.markmeynell.net/2020/10/02/o-tempora-o-mores-evangelici-2-hes-behind-you/>, accessed 10 October 2021.

they actually are, 'fruitless deeds of darkness' (Ephesians 5:11), and we should have nothing whatsoever to do with them. They are demonic, dehumanizing and have no place at all in the kingdom of light.

Once it has been established that a leader can extend or override the formal structure of authority, governance and accountability, sooner or later it becomes common and goes unremarked. The organization may still say 'accountable, plural and transparent' on the tin, but in reality the mechanisms are no longer functioning and have been replaced by coercive control.

7

The most serious abuses of power and position

Dear friends . . . I felt I had to write and urge you to contend for the faith that was once for all entrusted to the saints. For certain men whose condemnation was written about long ago have secretly slipped in among you. They are godless men, who change the grace of our God into a licence for immorality and deny Jesus Christ our only Sovereign and Lord.
(Jude 3–4)

There was no doubt who was the boss at the church – Seb, the minister. 'You took me on to see new people join the church,' he would say to the deacons, 'and they have. Fifty per cent growth in three years means my strategy is the right one.'

Privately, however, Seb bullied people. He would see them one to one and leave them in no doubt that not only was it was crucial for them to back him, but he couldn't work with leaders who wouldn't. The slightest hint at departure from his party line was met first with humiliating put-downs and then accusations of disloyalty. Seb was correct – people had joined the church. His ministry was outwardly attractive and dynamic to people who didn't know him. But it was also the case that some long-standing members had left, and their reasons were never reported to the wider church.

Finally, a family went to see one of the deacons and told him they were thinking about leaving, after a particularly bruising off-the-record encounter with Seb. They wanted to avoid doing so if at all possible, but if not it should be done in the right way. They asked the deacon if he would be willing to mediate in a meeting with Seb in which they expressed their concerns. For a long time Seb simply ignored the request, unwilling to allow concerns about him to be expressed in the presence of a third party. However, the deacon raised it more widely in personal emails to his colleagues, and at the next deacons' meeting the group insisted that Seb meet with the family and the proceedings should be chaired by the deacon.

Seb reluctantly agreed, but at the meeting he flatly denied the couple's concerns. He did admit he had delayed having a meeting due to over-busyness, for which he apologized, hoping that they could all move on constructively together. In response they said how sorry they were that things had got to the point where they had felt they needed to share with the deacon.

Seb followed up the meeting with a letter to the family, copied to all the deacons, saying how he had apologized to them for his over-busyness, and that they had apologized for gossiping and disloyalty, which had damaged him and the church. The family responded that they had not been disloyal, that expressing concerns privately to a member of the leadership was not gossiping, and that they apologized for neither. The deacon who chaired the meeting supported them and now he too became the target of repeated claims of dis-loyalty and gossip, for having shared the family's concerns with the deacons behind Seb's back.

Seb demanded an apology for the abusive way he had been spoken about and for being forced into a course of action he found demeaning and damaging to his reputation. He made it clear that the deacon must either apologize or stand down, or Seb himself would leave. Believing that it would be the least damaging option, the deacon crafted an apology, even though he knew he had nothing to apolo-gize for.

In the following Sunday service, Seb told the church that there had been terrible tensions among the leadership team due to gossip and a lack of commitment to team confidentiality, but that an apology had been received. He then proceeded to read it out to the church in the deacon's presence, and posted it on social media.

Seb is a bully who works by isolating people. He uses apparent successes as a shield to deflect criticisms and concerns. When unable to isolate the family in question he resorted to a catalogue of well-known abusive tactics: trying to extract false apologies that he presents as indications of more serious offences by others, binary choices that threaten to damage the church if he doesn't get his way, knowledge that soft-hearted people will usually back down for the sake of peace in the church, and use of his public platforms to demean anyone he finds a threat, while presenting himself as a victim of disloyalty and ungodly gossip. The family's future in the church and the deacon's place on the leadership team seem very doubtful. The Sebs of this world don't make it easy for people to stay once they have dared to challenge them.

The list of sinful, immoral, manipulative and coercive behaviours at the end of the last chapter shows that leaders can use position and power to build themselves up and tear others down to a terrible degree, well before getting to Stage 5. Nevertheless, it is worthwhile retaining a final category for the worst misuse of position and power, because there are some discernible features that are not present in the other categories.

The threshold between Stages 3 and 4 (other-serving and self-serving) might *just possibly* be crossed without full awareness or understanding of what is happening, perhaps with the tacit acquiescence of those being led. This blindness does not absolve leaders from responsibility, but it is distinct from Stage 5, which I am labelling 'the most serious abuses'. Those who operate in this category are not merely acting unwisely and in ungodly ways. They are deliberately using pastoral authority for their own sake, causing harm to others. They are also very clearly breaking biblical commands – at the very least against lying, but possibly also against sexual sin, violence and oppression – even though they will still find rationalizations or defences for their behaviour.

We have seen some of the ways leaders create power imbalances and set them in stone by capturing leadership cultures and structures. Now the power imbalance is used not to set people free in their service of God, but to dominate them through position, platform, public profile and private intimidation, forcing them to comply. It is a heinous abuse of trust and office.

It may be that leaders simply embrace the ethical standards of wider society, disregarding the fact that our standards as Christians are meant to be higher. We recognize as sinful certain behaviours that are not always disapproved of or illegal in the world; for example, power politics; various emotional, physical and social behaviours; consensual sex outside marriage; unreported financial or other gifts, or forcing leaders' wills on to the conscience of others. Such behaviours might be common, perhaps even seeming consensual (or at least accepted), in the world but must not be allowed to take root in churches.

Manipulative leaders might get their victims to 'buy in' to their treatment – for example, when they demand crippling financial giving with which their victims are in emotional or theological agreement at least (or are swept along by the tide of everyone else seeming to be in agreement). The fact that victims may engage in it in some sense willingly does not remove the charge of ungodly abuse from the leader.

Neither are leaders absolved when their ungodly actions are apparently consensual and not illegal; for example, as in the case of an affair. The fact that another person does not feel abused, or even claims to be OK with being used, does not mean leaders are not sinning against the Lord, his church and individuals. Genuine consent may also be compromised because of the power imbalance due to the involvement of leaders. It is akin to a teacher justifying being romantically or sexually involved with a pupil. Even with seemingly willing co-operation, the leader is still guilty of misusing position and power, as well as of other sin. Abuse of authority and power is an area in which churches must exercise, and be seen to exercise, zero tolerance. We do not accept ungodly behaviour – neither that which is scandalous to the watching world, nor even any that might be normal in the world.

Sinful behaviours frequently have sinful justifying teachings attached to them that actively promote evil, subtly downplay and excuse it or misdirect attention elsewhere. The church in Thyatira was tolerating a false teacher who misled people into immorality. In his letter to them in Revelation 2, the risen Lord Jesus did not say, 'Have a quiet word with her now and again, but don't rock the boat. Nobody wants a turbulent church life.' No! He told the whole church to 'repent of her immorality . . . Satan's so-called deep secrets', or they would be judged along with her, because 'I am he who searches hearts and minds' (see verses 20–25). There is sometimes genuine guilt by association! Not only will Jesus himself have nothing to do with evil, but he will also not put up with churches tolerating it either. In Jude's powerful rebuke quoted at the start of this chapter, to tolerate evil is to change grace into a licence for immorality and to deny the lordship of Jesus.

Features

The pathway into abuse is followed when leaders discard legitimate authority, manipulating the system so as to become impervious to scrutiny or accountability. This trajectory promotes a leadership culture in which leaders gather power, promote secrecy and in-crowds, and minimize the controls and safeguards surrounding themselves. Pastoral authority, devoid of biblical safeguards and exercised without Christ-like servant character and humility, has terrifying opportunities for abuse.

In Stage 5, leaders force others to be complicit in their own harm. This might be whole churches or groups, or individuals within a church and possibly those dear to them. It is systematic and sustained, and usually against the will or better judgement of their victims. More instances of abuse are coming to light, both historical and contemporary. The internet is providing some victims and survivors with a platform to finally break free from abusers and to challenge abusive leaders and cultures. It is revealing how common it is for victims to have no support or means to pursue grievances against powerful leaders. Indeed, a chief feature of abusers is that they isolate and act against the relatively powerless and defenceless, ensuring they won't be believed and can't get help.

Compliance is compelled by psychological control, institutional pressure, enforcement, inducements, threats and sanctions. The norms of transparency and accountability are entirely lacking. If there is plural leadership, it is likely they are all complicit in defending the most abusive leaders and maintaining the culture and structure that allows them to continue to act. This is not to say that all of their associates are themselves intentionally abusive. Coercive leaders greatly benefit from having some winsome 'good cops' around to improve their veneer of legitimacy, who themselves may also become victims to some degree.

More subtly (and deniably) corruption can happen at the level of tribes and cultures also, including denominations, groupings within denominations, church-planting and other homogenous networks, parachurch organizations, camps and the like. Indeed, anywhere coercive leaders can create a bubble or echo chamber. I agree with Paul Coulter's perceptive comment:

A great weakness of tribes is that they create echo chambers where only the concerns of those who define the tribe's boundaries are cause for expulsion. Furthermore, expulsion from a tribe seldom leads to someone being unable to form a new one or hook up with another or carry on their bad behaviour with the same people as before, just outside the tribe.[1]

When corrupted, tribes can have a terrible, systemic, gullible blindness to illegitimate behaviour, providing tribal covering and protection to people who are trusted simply because they are 'one of us'. I will say more about this in chapter 12.

At the smaller level of a local church or organization, corruption of plural leadership becomes even more likely when the inner circle includes married couples. I am not suggesting that family members should never become leaders together. It may be inevitable, especially in small churches and organizations, or in the early stages of a church plant. But when leadership structures are dominated by intimate family relationships, it can allow leaders to act with impunity, because decision-making can seldom be independent between them. Leadership decisions can effectively be made in the wrong context, over the meal table rather than in leadership meetings. When family relationships dominate leadership teams, much more work needs to be done to ensure transparency. It is not that due process is inevitably compromised, but who is going to make an allegation of abuse if the scrutineer is a family member? Abusive leaders always seek to remove scrutiny. A family-oriented inner circle makes it far easier.

The tools at the disposal of abusive leaders for enforcing obedience include dependency, belittling, isolation, domination, discrimination, exploitation, intimidation, insistence on loyalty, removing dissenters, binding people's consciences, threatening to cause trouble or to leave, blackmail, mental attack or even physical assault.

A common starting point is domination of time and relationships. This can begin as a call to total commitment to the mission of the gospel. Or, rather, the mission of the gospel as the leader presents it. Napoleon is supposed to have said that the leader's role is to define

---

1 In private conversation.

reality, then give hope. Abusive leaders advance their view of reality and present their way as the only hope. In the process, they align the vision of the organization more and more closely with themselves personally, until the two become indistinguishable and they become indispensable. To question the leader is to question the vision, indeed the whole organization. Possibly even the gospel.

Others are then evaluated, rewarded or punished according to how closely they conform to the vision. Time, money, loyalty and obedience become key indicators of commitment. Leaders set themselves up in the place God should have in people's lives, suppressing personal decision-making. External influences that might act as warnings or corrections are reduced and removed, methodically ensuring that involvement in the internal life of the community becomes the entire focus of existence and identity for the abused.

Abuse cannot persist in the light, so abusers also become experts at underhanded concealment and cover-up, sometimes accompanied by threats. They are adept at deflecting criticism, and will do anything to avoid impartial scrutiny. This includes silencing contrary views, misleading, lying, denial, harassment, defaming or removing opponents, and controlling systems to ensure behaviour cannot be reported and the abused won't be heard. Examples of the latter can include:

- making it impossible for anyone to accurately evaluate their leadership practice, or denying that anyone else has the skill or right;
- overseeing scrutinizing bodies, if their practice is to be scrutinized, thereby becoming their own referee;
- ensuring scrutiny that is unavoidable is carried out by those with less power in the structures: the junior, the inexperienced or those who are in some way beholden to the leader and who will not gainsay them;
- issuing explicit or implicit threats of church discipline or excommunication.

All of the above deceit is greatly helped, of course, by being popular and having a veneer of respectability and trustworthiness, gathering allies and creating alibis.

Cult-like leaders?

When leaders have crossed into Stage 5 they are fully aware that they have deliberately violated the limits of authority and moral behaviour. At Stage 4 abusive leaders will self-justify their behaviour, but in this worst category a leader knows that no self-justification will stand up to scrutiny. Therefore, all scrutiny must be avoided, either by removing it or by concealment.

The critical factors in discerning abuse of power and position are thoroughgoing safeguarding standards, principles and policies, training, statutory checks and reporting mechanisms. It is crucial that these are robust enough that they can be applied to the most senior leaders. Being most at risk, they need the most protection by careful standards.

Even these are not enough, however. Unless the church actively embraces and promotes both a culture of spiritual health among leaders (concern for their personal walk with God, the fruit of the Holy Spirit and habits of repentance), and a culture of good governance characterized by the combination of accountability, plurality and transparency, then policies and procedures are merely words on a piece of paper.

We have now surveyed the whole spectrum from godly, legitimate, accountable leadership that is wholly in the light, through to leadership that is abusive and may even begin to bear the hallmarks of a cult:

- charismatic leaders who have all the key ideas through a special degree of access to God;
- concentrated power and authority;

- totalizing vision, with penalties for dissent;
- heavy demands on commitment of time, energy and thought from followers;
- a culture that suppresses questioning;
- strong tribal boundaries that discourage transgression, with the threat of loss of community and friends.

Where leadership exhibits such features, it is unsurprising to find that common protocols for good practice and procedures for accountability are ignored or missing. There are no checks to prevent charismatic personalities from demanding total adherence to a vision that covers all aspects of life and unquestionable loyalty to themselves. They use this to feed themselves, making use of other people to their detriment and harm. It is the precise opposite of Christian pastoring. Such abuse of pastoral authority and callous disregard for integrity must be exposed and condemned in the clearest and strongest terms.

Part 3
WHAT NEXT?

8

What next for victims and survivors?

This is the verdict: Light has come into the world, but men loved darkness instead of light because their deeds were evil. Everyone who does evil hates the light, and will not come into the light for fear that his deeds will be exposed. But whoever lives by the truth comes into the light, so that it may be seen plainly that what he has done has been done through God.
(John 3:19–21)

We do not belong to the night or to the darkness. So then, let us not be like others, who are asleep, but let us be alert and self-controlled . . . But since we belong to the day, let us be self-controlled, putting on faith and love as a breastplate, and the hope of salvation as a helmet.
(1 Thessalonians 5:5b–6, 8)

Into the light

Jesus' verdict in John 3 could not be clearer: the reason people do things in the darkness is for fear of their evil being exposed. They love darkness and hate the light. When light is shone on their deeds, everyone can see that they are not acting in line with God. He is light. In him there is no darkness at all. The contention of this book is that illegitimate use of position and power, to whatever degree, major or minor, is done in the darkness. It doesn't stand up to scrutiny in the light. It isn't of God, regardless of how noble the motive. Without being melodramatic, behind misuse of power are principalities and powers of darkness. It is evil and we must take it with the utmost seriousness.

In this section we consider how we need to respond, ideally putting the brakes on before power goes wrong in churches, and recognizing that none of us are immune from heading down the slippery slope. We must also acknowledge that it is the vital and courageous exposure of historical and current cases of coercive leadership that is prompting much re-examination and fresh thinking in the UK at the time of writing. The question of how to respond is not abstract and must not be separated from questions of justice, repentance, restitution, discipline and culture reform. It is all too easy to focus on, say, the easy and objective work of repairing church policies without requiring personal repentance. Or to consider only the personal sins of individual leaders and not the cultural factors that enabled their abuse of power.

In the following chapters I will explore how churches, leaders and wider cultures and tribes might shine the light. However, I am conscious that some readers may well be victims/survivors (both those who are also now in church leadership and those who aren't but who are trying to make sense of these issues). It is important and appropriate, therefore, to also consider the situations of victims and whistle-blowers (who may already be victims, but will certainly become victims when they act).

What if I have been manipulated or abused by leaders?

While the main readership of this book will be leaders, it is quite possible that you are reading as a victim of abuse of pastoral authority, or that you have come to understand that you are as you have been reading. I am extremely sorry for your pain and distress. You know the crushing anguish of your church family ceasing to be a safe place;

of leaders you once trusted trying to control you, or having betrayed you. You have experienced your voice being silenced when you raised concerns. You may have lost friends or your church. Perhaps even your confidence in God has been rocked by the actions of a coercive leader.

We can spend months or even years looking at alternative explanations or justifications, or blaming ourselves, rather than come to the devastating conclusion that those we thought were principled, dependable and honest servants of God have broken that sacred trust and misused their power at our expense. The more devious our leaders are, the longer they can conceal their true intentions and behaviour. When what we once interpreted as love, friendship and pastoral care turns out to have been manipulative self-interest, the realization that we have been deceived and used can be overwhelming. Whether the coercive leader manipulates through undercover deceit or through overt bullying, finally acknowledging that this is the reality can leave us distrustful, ashamed and embarrassed at having been manipulated and used. We feel isolated, exploited, controlled, disempowered, weak and in danger.

You may be wrestling with a sense of abandonment and loss. Betrayal is utterly dreadful, leaving us not only grieving the loss of trust, but possibly berating ourselves for not seeing it sooner. We may even experience something akin to bereavement if we lose the community to which we have committed ourselves. One person who was forced to leave their church by a manipulative leader told me: 'I used to think it was fine for a person who didn't get on with the church leaders to find another church. After all, nobody was forcing them to come, and there are other churches. But then I was forced out by an abusive leader and I realized that I and my family were being exiled from our friends, our community where we had invested ourselves, and our Christian family. It was far more than simply leaving an organization and finding another one.'

Rejection and betrayal make it hard for us to trust people again, either leaders or meaningful community. If we choose to remain in the situation, emotional survival comes at the price of protecting ourselves *against*, and perhaps opposing, leaders who are trusted and followed by everyone else. This is rarely emotionally sustainable for very long, but even if we go to a new church after being harmed by leaders, we can struggle with self-doubt or fears of interacting with leadership, perhaps especially in settings of legitimate informal authority.

The road ahead

If this is you, you are at the start of a process of recovery. It may be a long and difficult one. While there may be much healing and better times in the future, nothing changes what has been done to you, or its ability to ambush your emotions in unexpected ways. Nevertheless, the journey always starts with recognizing trauma for what it is. You have a hard road and difficult decisions ahead of you, but you are no longer in denial.

I apologize that this section is short and deeply inadequate for your needs. I pray that it might encourage you to take the next step in getting the support you need. You may find it difficult to even describe what has happened and how it has affected you. It might be that expressing your experience in terms of 'trauma', 'loss' or 'betrayal' is something you haven't managed to do up to this point, but you now realize that these are appropriate words to describe your experience and feelings.

It may be helpful to think about the decisions you need to take in order to find support as four steps on a journey:

- Survival – finding a safe refuge.
- Understanding – gaining insight and clarity as to what has been done to you.
- Healing – processing what has happened from a stable place; being helped to integrate it into your story in ways that are less overshadowed by destructive turmoil.

- Justice – finding recourse and preventing abusive leaders from continuing to exercise power.

It needs to be said that if you are in immediate danger of physical or sexual harassment or violence, you need to get out straight away, certainly to supportive friends or family. If you believe a crime has been committed, you should seriously consider contacting the police.

The critical first thing is to find a place of safety. It is impossible to even begin to explore and talk about these things without it, or to consider next steps without turmoil and fear. If at all possible, start by seeking help from mature Christians who are outside your church, network or culture. If you simply don't have access to any because your entire context is unhealthy, then a call to a safeguarding body (e.g. Christian Safeguarding Services or Thirtyone:eight) may provide helpful advice.

Refuge is essential. Once we have it, understanding and healing become more possible over a period, though not guaranteed. Exploring trauma is never a one-off event but always a process, often a lengthy one. We are not objective when we have been victims of misuse of power. Once we are able to acknowledge to ourselves that we have been abused, it is easy for it to dominate every waking and sleeping thought, obsessively filling our entire horizon. It is very easy to become mired in turmoil, anger, hatred and over-defensiveness. These are entirely understandable, but serve neither our healing nor any subsequent pursuit of justice. We need to be well supported as we seek insight lest we find ourselves emotionally imprisoned and unable to escape from what has been done to us. Counselling is often extremely helpful for ordering our thoughts and feelings in a more constructive way, and certainly something to be considered.

The reason it is worth separating out the four areas is that they often happen on different timescales. The need for safety and survival is immediate and urgent. Understanding and healing occur over a longer period. Justice more commonly happens over the longest period of all, if we ever receive it – and that is not guaranteed. Sometimes we can feel that it is impossible to heal without receiving justice, and it is tempting, therefore, to try to address both at the same time. However, in many cases justice simply isn't forthcoming. I wish I could say otherwise. If we tie our recovery to it, not only does it leave us seeking healing and justice in the middle of our own turmoil, but it also leaves our emotional, psychological and spiritual health (and possibly our physical health) perpetually at the mercy of those who have wounded us. It is critical to avoid that if we can. Frequently those people have no interest in the justice that would help our recovery, because it would require them to own up to their actions, which they have no desire to do at all.

What if I'm not sure whether what I experienced was manipulation or abuse?

While in many cases manipulation and abuse are clear-cut, you might be working through confusion and turmoil in complex situations, and truth may be hard to discern. You might feel a boundary has been overstepped, but it feels difficult and fuzzy.

I'm extremely hesitant to introduce any caveats at all at this point. Abusive leaders can exploit ambiguity through gaslighting and DARVO, and I do not want to enable those tactics. I have seen a variety of conflicted situations in which different factors make it hard for people to make sense of what they have gone through:

- Where there are multiple competing narratives, in which everyone believes they are telling the truth. Perhaps an honest complainant makes sincere claims about abuse of power, which are then investigated, but the investigation rules them to be incorrect. The complainant, however, is resolute that the claims are true and is unsatisfied by the outcome. They may believe the process of investigation to be biased for not coming down on their side. It is easy to recast painful situations in such a way as to see ourselves exclusively in the role of victim or whistle-blower, when the reality may be more complicated.

- Where people find it impossible to believe that leaders who can show great kindness may also abuse their power.
- Where people interpret healthy church discipline, or even disagreement, as coercion.
- Where people interpret personality clash as sin. The situation becomes dominated not by investigation of specific sins but by bruised feelings. What matters is not what someone did or did not do but how others feel about them.
- Where people have been abused by powerful leaders, but also feel a degree of responsibility, perhaps knowing that they too have things of which they need to repent.
- Where there are complicit victims. Among the most complex and tortuous situations are where people (especially leaders) could have blown the whistle and are later criticized and held responsible for not having doing so, when at the time they were themselves victims. They remained silent not to protect the guilty (though it may have had that effect), but for the sake of personal survival, or simply not knowing what to do.

I recognize that these are incredibly sensitive issues in which enormous care, wisdom and prayer are needed. What they highlight are the vital importance of obtaining external perspective to help us not to leap to immediate conclusions. We need to acknowledge the frailty and fallibility of our own hearts and understanding, carefully examine ourselves as much as we are able, and value transparent, objective, external processes. If an investigation concludes to the dissatisfaction of one party but all can agree it was well conducted, there is some possibility of moving on, however limited and inadequate.

What next?

I am praying for you as I write this, that the Lord Jesus will draw close to you and pour out the oil of his healing in your life. In response to the wicked shepherds in Ezekiel, who cared for themselves and not for the flock, God said:

> I will rescue my flock from their mouths, and it will no longer be food for them. For this is what the Sovereign LORD says: I myself will search for my sheep and look after them . . . I myself will tend my sheep and make them lie down . . . I will search for the lost and bring back the strays. I will bind up the injured and strengthen the weak, but the sleek and the strong I will destroy. I will shepherd the flock with justice.
> (Ezekiel 34:10b–11, 15–16)

9

What next for whistle-blowers?

Humble yourselves, therefore, under God's mighty hand, that he may lift you up in due time. Cast all your anxiety on him because he cares for you. Be self-controlled and alert. Your enemy the devil prowls around like a roaring lion looking for someone to devour. Resist him, standing firm in the faith, because you know that your brothers throughout the world are undergoing the same kind of sufferings. And the God of all grace, who called you to his eternal glory in Christ, after you have suffered a little while, will himself restore you and make you strong, firm and steadfast. To him be the power for ever and ever. Amen.

(1 Peter 5:6–11)

It is uncommon for Christians to blow the whistle on misuse of power and authority. I don't believe this is usually out of lack of integrity. A feature of all abusive relationships is that people are slow to realize what is happening, and when the realization does dawn it may not be at all clear what can or should be done. Christian whistle-blowers are commonly the first people to see the ugliness behind the mask that self-serving leaders wear. They are likely to be confidentially minded people who are averse to sharing with others out of fear of trouncing someone's reputation, so they can find themselves processing things in isolation, stuck in a downward spiral of emotional turmoil and fear.

Whistle-blowers know that when they finally bring things to light, they will, in most cases, find themselves unprotected and incredibly vulnerable, even if successful. The risks inherent in challenging power are high and the disincentives clear. When the need to act becomes overwhelming and unavoidable, potential whistle-blowers may already have been badly treated. The abused are often less likely to confront abusers because they are already at the end of their resources and fearful of going through even more. They may have been silenced, ignored, threatened or gaslit, being made highly vulnerable in the process. Which is, of course, the point. In many instances it is simply far easier and less painful not to continue to put up with it, but just to walk away. But even when a person does blow the whistle, it is much easier for a well-defended leader to dismiss an already vulnerable victim as emotionally unstable or unreliable.

What are the disincentives?

1 Isolation

Misuse of power and position is commonly experienced or witnessed by lone individuals long before it comes to wider attention. This is not least because it is often directed against individuals rather than groups, and they don't see that the leader or culture is doing the same to others. These things happen in multiple, isolating silos, in any one of which the leader who is going wrong has the greater power. If abused individuals are isolated prior to bringing an accusation, they know they will be far more so once they do.

2 A disposition to forgiveness

Christians are (we hope) naturally given to forgiveness. This predisposes victims to question themselves first, perhaps assuming they are misreading the situation or missing information. They might be told they don't see the issues or are just wrong. Misuse of power may be excused as eccentricity, quirkiness, grumpiness or strong and robust leadership by defenders. While such character traits may not in themselves be abuse of power and position, they can provide cover for it. Coercive leaders always have defenders: 'That's just so-and-so's way. Don't worry about it.' Hence it is almost always a case of vulnerable individuals going up against a defended group. It is much easier to accept these explanations for the sake of a quiet life, rationalizing that it is better to put up with being hurt than make false accusations, especially if no-one will believe you or stand with you.

The flip side of this is holding on to the hope that matters may be correctable if you carry on working in the system rather than calling it out. Perhaps by remaining silent it might be possible to change or improve the situation and limit damage to others. I can understand the sense of duty and sacrifice underlying such a position, but I don't think it is wise or right for people to remain in situations of abusive leadership, and certainly not if it is sexual or physical. While Christians do have a general duty to be soft-hearted, forgiveness is dependent on repentance. To forgive in the absence of repentance is to validate sinful behaviour. And even when someone does genuinely repent, and forgiveness is appropriate, there should be no obligation to remain under their leadership – nor for them to remain in leadership.

3 Theological reasons

There are various theological reasons that will cause Christians to be slow to blow the whistle. Jesus tells us to let those who are without sin cast the first stone. Soft-hearted believers might be reluctant to blow the whistle because they know they are not without sin themselves. Perhaps they might reason, 'Maybe this is not my problem. After all, the Bible says that vengeance belongs to the Lord, and it is his job to repay injustice.' They might struggle with whether their motivation is really to expose evil in order to stop it, or to avenge themselves in order to punish it.

Of course, coercive leaders have plenty of convincing religious-sounding arguments to divert attention from their behaviour. You might be told that to rock the boat endangers the church or the mission of the gospel, and that to continue reveals a destructive and unchristian spirit; or that you should take the plank out of your own eye before criticizing others. I've met complainants who have been threatened with church discipline simply to silence them. These responses are little more than theological blackmail to deflect criticism from the ones who really are behaving in an unchristian manner.

And then the apostle Peter tells us to put away malice. By the time a potential whistle-blower has run out of other options there is a real chance that abuse has already created feelings of malice. In 1 Corinthians 4:12 we are told that when we are reviled, the Christian response is to bless, and 1 Corinthians 6 is clear about not taking other believers to court. If our Saviour was willing to be crucified for our salvation, perhaps we can reason that putting up with being bullied and victimized is just part of being a Christian.

Certainly, the desire to be like Jesus causes believers to put up with bad behaviour far longer than they would under other circumstances. We might harbour a fear that in fighting back we may become a mirror image of the very behaviour we are opposing. However, the Bible does not in any way teach us to endure wickedness in the church quietly. From beginning to end, it reveals how God loves righteousness and justice. Looking forward to Jesus, the psalmist says he will be joyously exalted for precisely that reason:

Your throne, O God, will last for ever and ever;
    a sceptre of justice will be the sceptre of your
        kingdom.
You love righteousness and hate wickedness;
    therefore God, your God, has set you above your
        companions
    by anointing you with the oil of joy.
(Psalm 45:6–7)

And the pastoral epistles are very clear about rebuking and exhorting from Scripture: 'All Scripture is God-breathed and is useful for teaching, rebuking, correcting and training in righteousness' (2 Timothy 3:16). This is for all Christians. There is no hint that leaders are exempt from exhortation, rebuke and correction. In fact, throughout the Bible, when the people stray from God it is always because the leaders refuse to listen to and obey God's Word. Far from being immune, they are more in need of godly rebuke and correction than anyone!

Fight or flight?

Most of us only blow the whistle when faced with no choice – once we decide that someone is abusing their power, either against us or others. Deciding to fight when we are at the end of our tether is a difficult choice. By the time someone reaches that last resort, the manipulative leader is likely to be well entrenched, while the whistle-blower is exhausted and desperate to walk away from it all and find a safe and settled refuge.

It is a big thing to have our illusions shattered, especially in relation to once-trusted leaders, our church community, our spiritual life or even God. Why stick around and get involved in the mud-slinging that is inevitable when abusive leaders are challenged? That will just damage us further. When faced with confronting coercive leaders, there is neither a level playing field nor fair play. We can guarantee we will get hurt.

This is just as true for Christian workers, church officers or employees. Being closer to a coercive leader – for example, on a church leadership team – may give them clearer insight into the situation, but seeing it more clearly does not make whistle-blowing easier. Often it makes it harder, as their livelihood might be on the line, especially if the abuser is their boss with the power to fire. One missionary said to me, 'My financial support is dependent on the church. If I blow the whistle my income may be switched off, and I may not be believed anyway. I feel trapped.' It is easy to sympathize. The very act of whistle-blowing presumes that the person, group or system being called to account is above us in terms of power dynamics.

Whistle-blowers are almost certainly going to find their character and judgement called into question. They and their family may lose friends or their social life, perhaps even their church community. It is common for people to come to the defence of the abuser rather than the whistle-blower. Flight is almost always the easier option.

The consequences of whistle-blowing

It is vital in the mind of the power-abusing leader that the truth must not emerge. Abusers may begin with stalling tactics, especially if the complainant is in some position of trust and respect, and able to hold their own for a bit. If the can is kicked down the road for long enough, there is a chance that the accuser will be removed, by causing them to crumble in a war of attrition and to leave before they get anywhere.

The longer the complainant persists, however, the more desperate abusive leaders become. The closer their behaviour gets to being exposed to the light of examination, the more unpleasant it becomes for the whistle-blower. To discourage truth-telling, the potential consequences need to be severe:

- being disbelieved or labelled an agitator, gossip, untrustworthy or even a traitor;
- fear of receiving retaliation, emotional abuse or threats from coercive leaders or their supporters;
- being erased, having to witness the facts of the matter being altered and airbrushed out by the powerful abusing party;

- being gaslit (remember DARVO: deny anything is wrong, attack the challenger, reverse victim and offender);
- jeopardizing your own position in the church community, and that of your family (if challenging causes you to end up in the wilderness without doing any good, what's the point?);
- jeopardizing friendships or putting friends in similar jeopardy – not wanting people to distance themselves from you because they fear the consequences for themselves if they don't;
- fear of unleashing unintended consequences that might damage the cause of the gospel;
- fear that acting might make things worse rather than better and therefore it is better to settle for the lesser of evils;
- fear that taking responsibility will result in conflict that will force you, if unsuccessful, to leave the church or organization (or possibly even if successful, if enough defenders of the coercive leader make it too unpleasant for you to remain);
- fear that lifting the lid might mean the person in question also gets blamed for all kinds of other things they're not guilty of, this world being as unnuanced as it is;
- fear that you might be the one who removes someone's livelihood, house, means to support their family or future employment;
- fear of continuing to remain under the authority of leaders you no longer trust or who see you as the opposition.

All of this takes place in an environment that offers little hope of protection, in which we may experience a strong incentive to be deliberately blind. We can persuade ourselves that the person couldn't possibly be behaving like *that*. Any other explanation is preferable to the pain and loss we will experience if it is true. We can pre-decide the best possible and least destructive explanation for their behaviour and then, working backwards, reinterpret what we have experienced in the light of it. Once we have decided what the situation *must* be or *could not* be, confirmation bias does the rest to make us remain silent. This always leaves the power-abusers in position.

It is also possible to rationalize that we would accept the sacrifice of speaking out, provided it was in the wider interests of the fellowship to do so. But here the concern for self-protection and trying to figure out how best to protect the church overlap in complicated and confusing ways. It is rarely easy to work out when a leader's behaviour ceases to be a one-off, or a series of understandable mistakes that should be handled quietly for the good of all, but rather should be viewed as a symptom of deeper failings that need to be exposed.

When the stakes are this high it is extremely tempting to convince ourselves that examination and exposure risks hurting more people than it helps. All responsible Christians have a profound aversion to destabilizing churches. Do we really want to wave a red flag if there is a risk that by doing so we leave the church a smoking ruin? In any given instance it is easier to conclude that something doesn't warrant taking action than to decide that this is the final crossed boundary that does. Like the proverbial frog, we boil by degrees.

What must we do?

The questions potential whistle-blowers have to answer for themselves, with much prayer, are: what is my responsibility before the Lord? What, in good conscience, *must* I do? What may I not do without my conscience condemning me? Beyond these are questions of appropriate channels and means, but these are the primary questions.

One of the painful costs for church officers in this situation is having to move away from unequivocally supporting the team and to dissent from collective responsibility. Under normal circumstances team-working and collective responsibility (the coming to shared decisions that are presented to the church with a united front) are critical for elders to fulfil their responsibilities. But when things are going wrong at leadership level it cannot be maintained. Now an elder must go against natural instinct instead. However uncomfortable, continuing to support leaders under those circumstances is no longer to uphold the trust of the church but to betray it.

However, breaking ranks from the collective decisions of the rest of the leadership is almost bound to be branded as hostility or betrayal by abusive leaders. Paradoxically, the point at which someone feels they need to blow the whistle is also the point at which calls for collective responsibility are likely to dramatically intensify, not for the sake of healthy team working but as an emotionally manipulative tool to censor and silence dissent.

I believe it is critical not to keep things entirely to yourself, especially if you are going up against a powerful group or an institution. Sometimes there is a fine line between sharing and gossip, but the power imbalances between lone whistle-blowers and power-abusing leaders can be so great as to render sole complainants impotent even before they speak, and to damage them mightily afterwards. You need the protection of prayerful people who will listen carefully without necessarily just agreeing with you. Whistle-blowers need a lot of support and scaffolding around them. You need to bear in mind that by inviting people to support you, you may be implicating them in any backlash, but if you can find godly people, they will willingly embrace the cost.

It is well worth preparing carefully what you will and will not say, and how you will say it. When everything comes out and extreme emotions are at play, this will help you to remain accountable to godly decisions and words that you prepared beforehand, rather than giving in to your anger in the heat of the moment. Moreover, whistle-blowing frequently has unintended consequences, and not always godly and positive ones. One specific area that I have seen more than once is when other people seize on the blowing of the whistle and use situations of real abuse to try to bring down innocent leaders, groups and structures they don't like, quite divorced from the intention of the original whistle-blower. Whistle-blowers should not refrain from acting because of potential unknown consequences, nor are they responsible for the ungodly actions of others. However, they can be impugned as the person who enabled them, so having wise counsel that might help foresee possible pitfalls, and support when they arise, is invaluable.

As with any serious matter of discipleship, it is critical to count the potential cost to yourself and your family and lift it up to the Lord in prayer. That cost is likely to be high. I wish I could tell you otherwise. I am praying for you as I write this, especially if you are deciding right now whether to fight or flee. The cruel reality is that abusive leaders often win, but even if they don't the cost to the whistle-blower is extreme. However, once you are persuaded that you should blow the whistle, the cost to your conscience of not doing so will be longer-term and higher still, so: 'Trust in the LORD with all your heart and lean not on your own understanding; in all your ways acknowledge him, and he will make your paths straight' (Proverbs 3:5–6).

10

What next for leaders?

To the elders among you, I appeal as a fellow-elder, a witness of Christ's sufferings and one who also will share in the glory to be revealed: Be shepherds of God's flock that is under your care, serving as overseers – not because you must, but because you are willing, as God wants you to be; not greedy for money, but eager to serve; not lording it over those entrusted to you, but being examples to the flock. And when the Chief Shepherd appears, you will receive the crown of glory that will never fade away.

(1 Peter 5:1–4)

Examine yourselves to see whether you are in the faith; test yourselves.

(2 Corinthians 13:5)

Unexamined leaders

A counsellor I used to visit once commented that Christian leaders seem very reluctant to pause and examine themselves. Moreover, they have a most convenient excuse for not doing so: they just don't have time because there is always more ministry to do.

If we as leaders are poor at self-examination, we can be poorer still at submitting ourselves to examination, evaluation and review from others. In fact, it is common to end up entirely unexamined in ministry or, if there is examination, for it not to be in conjunction with or responsible to the local church, but conducted by some external body such as a diocese or presbytery. For independent churches and church-planting movements that affirm the authority of local church eldership, the challenge is that the sending church or planting network might play a validating or certifying function but offer little by way of accountability mechanisms if local leaders become coercive.

Living unobserved lives in ministry is incredibly dangerous. We are fallen people. None of us is so sanctified that we could not be guilty of misuse of power and position. Being our own judge ensures that we can never be sure if we are on a healthy trajectory or not, and it leaves us unable to handle challenges to our use of position in a constructive, rather than defensive, way.

One question that demonstrates integrity is: how do I know I am using my power in a way that honours God and serves others, and is it an expression of the fruit of the Holy Spirit?[1] An even more important question to make us honest about ourselves is: how would I know if I wasn't?

Scripture passages that speak about leadership character and wise practice frequently provide a contrast with bad practice. This is incredibly helpful because, as we have seen, manipulative leaders can so easily use the good things they are doing to minimize or justify the bad. James 3 is a good example, where wise leadership is described as exhibiting a good life with deeds done in humility, pure, peace-loving, considerate, submissive, full of mercy and good fruit, impartial, sincere, and keeping careful reign over our tongue. It echoes the fruit of the Holy Spirit in Galatians, as applied to leadership. And just as the fruit of the Spirit is contrasted with symptoms of ungodliness, so James contrasts wise leadership with boastfulness, cursing, envy, selfish ambition and denial of the truth, which cause disorder and every evil practice.

---

1   Chris Green provides some excellent evaluative questions in this blog post at: <www.ministrynutsandbolts.com/2020/02/11/leadership-is-never-an-excuse/>, accessed 10 October 2021.

The authenticity of godly leadership is not revealed by the good things alone. It is seen both in what it *is* and in what it *isn't*. Not merely in what it embraces, but by what it actively puts to death. Commenting on the works of the flesh in Galatians 5, Chris Green says:

> It should be a red flag for any pastor, group of elders, presbytery, or bishop (depending on your ecclesiology) when we hear stories about a church which is marked by those kinds of behaviours. Those will be the dark side of any Christian and are to be put to death. Every personality type can have an expression of all of those, and we are wise if we know that about ourselves. Talk about them, be aware of them, challenge and be challenged.[2]

The Pastoral Epistles, similarly, are clear that leaders are evaluated both against positive criteria and what they are *not* like. They should:

- be above reproach (and not merely have an *appearance* of being above reproach);
- be the husband of one wife;
- be temperate;
- be self-controlled;
- be worthy of respect;
- be hospitable;
- be able to teach;
- not be given to drunkenness;
- not be violent;
- be gentle;
- not be quarrelsome;
- not be a lover of money;
- be able to manage own family well;

---

2 See note 1 above.

- not be a recent convert who might find leadership tempts them to be conceited;
- be in possession of a good reputation with outsiders;
- be sincere;
- be able to hold the deep truths of the faith with a clear conscience;
- be able to correctly handle the word of truth;
- not be indulging in godless chatter.

If we read such a list thinking, 'How can I evade this and make sure nobody knows what I am really like?' rather than, 'How can I live in repentance and faith, confessing and more closely conforming to this vision of godly leadership?' then our hearts are being exposed by God's Word. We may be able to avoid scrutiny by other people, but he is the chief evaluator and nothing is hidden from him: 'Do your best to present yourself to God as one approved, a workman who does not need to be ashamed and who correctly handles the word of truth' (2 Timothy 2:15).

No leader is perfect. The barometer is not whether we are sin free, but rather whether we receive these biblical criteria as good, and desire to submit to God, walking in repentance and faith. Yet this kind of exposure of leaders to biblical evaluation is rare, either prior to or during their leadership.

Being honest about ourselves

By the time leaders have started to serve themselves, these biblical criteria are probably something they want to avoid rather than embrace anyway. Many do not fall into that category, however, and are keen to make changes to ensure they never do. But they face another problem, which is that almost all Christian workers are poor at being honest about themselves and processing these things on their own.

It is far from easy to identify trustworthy people with whom we can share at sufficient depth that they are able to help us see our faults without condemning us. The people we choose as advisors, counsellors, professional supervisors or spiritual directors are some of the most important decisions we can ever make. Such people are worth their weight in gold. It is no surprise that good rulers and bad in the Bible can often be distinguished according to whether they surrounded themselves with wise or foolish counsel. A critical tell-tale warning metric for all Christian leaders is whether we have anyone who can correct us, and how open and accessible we are to receiving it. Who could, and would, legitimately and constructively challenge us for our good if they thought we were going wrong?

The reason we as leaders are bad when it comes to evaluation is because it is evaluating our *selves*. There is a fine line between someone's work in Christian ministry and that person's life, especially if the leadership role has been allowed to become all-consuming, forming the foundation of affirmation and identity. Hence many of our more dangerous tendencies are flip sides of more healthy parts of our calling and spiritual gifts. See Table 1 on page 116.

The factors that tip leaders from the positive side to the negative include unjustified views of their gifts and abilities (possibly including a theology of ordination/anointing), or unrealistic expectations that provoke fear. It can be born out of pride or low self-esteem, both of which are compounded in different ways by lack of plural leadership, isolation and fear of repentance.

I want to remain godly

We can never afford to let our guard down in these areas, because the desire for control is unrelenting. As the apostle Paul put it: 'Examine yourselves to see whether you are in the faith; test yourselves' (2 Corinthians 13:5). In other words, we should pursue self-awareness with regard to godly leadership practice.

Table 1 Positive and negative sides of calling and gifting

Positive	Negative
I am recognized by the church as having God-given gifts for leadership.	Disagreeing with me is disagreeing with God's plan.
I am gifted and trained.	Nobody else has this training or gifting and therefore no-one can hold me accountable or carry out any part of my responsibilities. I am threatened when anyone does part of my job better than I do.
I am experienced and can therefore more naturally see what needs to be done.	I define the reality, the mission, the means and the ends. Others need to listen to my experience, not the other way around.
The church needs vibrant leadership.	I need to be strong and robust even if others are uncertain or opposed, otherwise I am not being a good leader.
I have good intentions and no concerns about my own integrity.	I am justified in deciding on and using unaccountable means.
I am dedicated to serving others.	Other people must follow me out of respect for my service.
I and my family make significant sacrifices to do this work.	We should have some status in this community that compensates for the sacrifices we make.
I am engaged in many activities that provide measures of success in my work.	I have an impoverished prayer life because the prayer life of leaders is not something visible that is valued by others.

How do we do this? The critical first step is to have the humility to admit that we are not immune from the dangers, and then to actively invite scrutiny. We must be upfront about this with people. Many in churches wrongly assume that leaders, by dint of having been authorized, are no longer in danger. We need to correct this misunderstanding and find ways in practice to:

- actively seek checks and balances on our leadership;
- be clear with church officers, and maybe the whole church, about the dangers of position and power, and that we are not immune to them;
- make it easy for people to tell us if we are going wrong;
- ensure that we have functioning personal and organizational accountability;
- insist on procedures, policies and practices that expose us to the light.

King David was blessed to have a Nathan to challenge him after the event. We can only speculate what might have happened had he had a Nathan-type conversation before the event. Maybe he did – his chief advisor Ahithophel's wisdom was said to be like the voice of God (2 Samuel 16:23), but his advice counted for nothing when David decided he wanted Ahithophel's granddaughter Bathsheba (2 Samuel 11). We can all find ways of avoiding wise counsel we would rather not hear.

What safeguards do you need? What would be strong enough to guard you and others against your worst self? Leaders require trust-worthy people and structures gathered around them to responsibly keep a close eye on them; those who will put their finger on things for their own good. Who are your accountability team who are invited to do so, affirmed in it, and to whom you will genuinely listen when they have hard things to say? As I have mentioned before, it is valuable to have counsel from outside your local church as well as from within (with the proviso that the external party is committed to respecting the polity of the church, rather than overriding it). If the answer is that you are functionally accountable to nobody, then you are in grave danger.

Other helpful questions include:

- Do I genuinely put the interests of others first, considering them better than myself (Philippians 2:3–4)?
- Do I co-opt people who will support me unthinkingly?
- Do I welcome review of my leadership?
- Do I insist that church policies and procedures are strong and clear enough to hold me accountable?
- Do I willingly recuse myself when I have a conflict of interest?
- Do I make myself transparent with team or church officers?
- Do I enfranchise and equip people to play a full part in the team, or am I threatened when others are more gifted or competent than I am?
- Do I have to appear successful to the church to protect myself from feelings of vulnerability or inadequacy?
- Do I finally get my way in all decisions, or are there times when I accede to others?
- Am I ever tempted to lie to cover up mistakes, or deceive in order to disguise how I am trying to get my own way?
- Am I ever tempted to use DARVO defences (deny, attack, reverse victim and offender) to protect myself?
- If someone raises a serious issue about my leadership practice or integrity, is my instinct to listen, to excuse myself, or to silence or refuse to interact with them? Will they get a fair hearing or not?
- In such circumstances would I welcome impartial and independent scrutiny, and possibly arbitration? Or would I try to determine how the adjudication process works, making sure any investigation is biased to my own advantage?

Leaders who want to avoid the slippery slope will be the most proactive in establishing healthy accountability and will lead the way on good policies and building a transparent culture.

What if I realize I've gone wrong?

Whether we are accountable to people or not can often reveal whether we are accountable to God. Do you have anyone to whom you are genuinely, functionally accountable for your leadership? If the answer, in practice, is no then you are probably leading without accountability to God either. You may well have already travelled too far down the slippery slope. I plead with you to be honest with yourself about this. Without accountability you may be misusing your power and exceeding your authority, even without knowing it. The Lord has given a trust to leaders that they do not get to exercise in splendid isolation.

Can you be fairly challenged? The revealing question would be whether a responsible and thoughtful person who was concerned about your leadership could raise questions concerning your practice or integrity and get an impartial and independent hearing. If doing so would potentially have negative consequences for them, you already know that you are leading from a place of ungodliness. It is possible that the Lord is convicting you even as you read this. You need to repent, at the very least of having made yourself your own adjudicator.

Recognition is the vital first step in the right direction. If you sense a reluctance to explore further, what is the source of it? You need to identify and name why continuing to live in denial seems the easier path. Is it that you will have to forsake the protection or advantages that go with the power you have gained? Is it fear that those you have wronged may seek to gain the upper hand over you? Is it that you feel your position, reputation, perception of ability to do your job or your livelihood may be threatened?

It is easy to persuade ourselves that the least painful option is to carry on covering up. We can even justify not coming into the light on the grounds that it would be too painful for others, discouraging for the church or damaging to the reputation of Christ were we to do so. In fact, what we are really worried about is the loss we will suffer – the destruction of our credibility and perhaps our ministry – and the knowledge that we will need to submit ourselves to the judgement of others and repent to those we have damaged.

Pride is a fearful demotivator to repentance and taking responsibility. However, covering up leads into a permanent, cumulative cycle of deceit, which becomes ever harder to break out of because the consequences of doing so only ever get more catastrophic over time.

When confronted with his sin, King Saul tried to look repentant while carrying on with an unchanged heart (1 Samuel 15). Repentance for him was a surface matter to keep people happy. It was the equivalent of 'I am sorry if . . .', a formula which commonly contains no repentance at all. But false repentance only keeps us trapped. True repentance frees us to stop making excuses, turn back to God and begin to make amends to those we have wronged and broken.

The book of James makes it clear that deeds done in humility reflect the wisdom of heaven: they are pure, peace-loving, considerate, submissive, full of mercy and good fruit, impartial and sincere, full of righteousness. This is the challenge for leaders who have gone wrong: is this wisdom what you now want to embrace? If so, you can no longer hang on to the self-righteous 'wisdom' that is from the devil – ambition, envy, boastfulness or denial of the truth (James 3:13–18).

There is little that Satan hates more than godly repentance. He knows how foundational it is to the Christian life and to godly leadership. He will do anything to stop us confessing our sin and being forgiven. He well knows that 'Godly sorrow brings repentance that leads to salvation and leaves no regret, but worldly sorrow brings death' (2 Corinthians 7:10). He will provide any distraction, raise every fear, offer us even more seductive power and control, or even make us think that repentance will cause us to die, so long as he can keep us enslaved.

Repentance always involves other people, both those who can help us repent and those to whom we need to repent. The further we have moved into illegitimate or abusive leadership, the more we need others to help us work through the consequences of repentance, reparation and restoration. The greater the power differential with those we have wronged, the more important mediation and trusted third parties become.

It must be said that third parties have to be able to adjudicate whether it is appropriate for us to remain in Christian leadership, or in our current position. If we have abused our position of trust but admit no possibility of needing to step down, there is no chance of meaningful repentance. Hard though it may be to hear, we have neither a God-given right to remain in leadership nor to be our own referee. And we cannot merely assume that genuine repentance and forgiveness should automatically put someone on a track back into leadership (at least on the same timescale as the repentance). Even if they are sorry, leaders who have misused their power cannot assume the right to be trusted with leadership again, nor that they wouldn't be tempted in the same way in future. I cannot say strongly enough: apart from the Lord, nobody has an inalienable right to exercise power and authority in the kingdom of God.

I urge you, if the Lord is convicting you as you read, do not delay. These things may be terrifyingly difficult to face, but you need to stop having fellowship with fruitless deeds of darkness. You are damaging others and destroying your own peace and joy in God by refusing to repent or by protecting your own position. You are not serving the work of the gospel, however much you think you are, because it doesn't advance through untruth. Whatever you think you gain by not repenting, it is a lie. Yes, repentance is hard, but it reveals that you are honest. The voices telling you not to do it are deceiving you.

> Create in me a pure heart, O God, and renew a steadfast spirit within me.
> Do not cast me from your presence or take your Holy Spirit from me.
> Restore to me the joy of your salvation and grant me a willing spirit, to sustain me.
> (Psalm 51:10–12)

11

What next for churches?

Jesus knew that the Father had put all things under his power, and that he had come from God and was returning to God; so he got up from the meal, took off his outer clothing and wrapped a towel round his waist. After that, he poured water into a basin and began to wash his disciples' feet, drying them with the towel that was wrapped round him.
(John 13:3–5)

Churches have personalities

We come now to churches. It can be extremely difficult for churches and leadership teams to become more aware of the underlying expectations and patterns of their leadership. This is especially true regarding accountability for the most senior minister.

Churches have paradigms that are rarely examined:

> organizations have personalities. As people become involved, they are socialized into the ways of the organization's system. Participants' actions and attitudes begin to mirror subtle rituals and practices reflecting expectations for proper conduct . . . Organizational culture can be defined as 'the way we do things around here'.[1]

Our relational environment, values, history, expectations, habits and community narratives, and our understanding, theology and

---

1 Bob Burns, Tasha D. Chapman and Donald C. Guthrie, *The Politics of Ministry: Navigating Power Dynamics and Negotiating Interests* (Illinois: IVP, 2019), 154.

practice of leadership are like the air we breathe. We participate without thinking twice about them. But we *need* to think about them because, unexamined, our cultural norms can themselves become coercive. For example, if a church embraces a leadership paradigm that is more reflective of commerce or the military than it is of Jesus washing his disciples' feet, it will believe leadership is mostly about efficient organization with a chain of command and certain skills for delivering measurable outcomes.

Churches sometimes abuse leaders before leaders abuse their position

Before exploring how churches can better protect themselves against unhealthy use of leadership power, I want to describe three ways in which an unhealthy church can contribute to godly leaders beginning to go astray. Once again, to describe these dynamics is not to make excuses for abuse of power, or to minimize individual responsibility.

1 A visible-results culture

Pressure to produce visible results can diminish the spiritual depth that should mark a Christian leader. Ask many paid Christian leaders what their job description is and they will reply, 'Prayer and ministry of the word.' Ask the church what it thinks leaders' jobs entail, however, and you will rarely hear prayer mentioned, because it is unseen. Leaders who acquiesce to the priority of visible results can find their prayer life squeezed out of them, because the people value what they can see, not imperceptible spiritual benefits. This is amplified where leaders are not expected to equip and support others in their ministries in the body of Christ, but are in fact paid to do the ministry of the whole body. Needless to say, this is impossible. If not very careful, leaders can be affirmed for things that come at the expense of spiritual depth and prayer. This in turn can lead to . . .

2 A hyper-committed culture

If there is one factor in particular that fuels domination in a church context, I would probably identify a culture of hyper-commitment.

A critical factor to be aware of is that the work and life patterns of many Christian leaders are not spiritually healthy. Many believe, rightly or wrongly, that the expectations on them are sufficiently high that they cannot carry out their responsibilities in a way that healthily integrates life, home, ministry and their spiritual life. Many feel they have no choice but to make sacrifices in home life to make church work. When churches grow numerically it is unusual for their leadership team to grow proportionately and prospectively to need, eroding leaders' capacity till their load exceeds their limits. For most ministers this means more and more evening meetings, because that is the only time church volunteers can meet. Those who are married start passing their spouse like ships in the night. The spouse can feel afraid to insist on change lest it produce despair in their partner, who feels trapped and unable to change the culture, disapproval from the church, or even a sense of being unfaithful to God. When leaders stop leading out of the love of God in the church, it may also be that the perceived demands have prevented them living in the love of God at home a long time before.

Not only is it common to find many people in ministry working three-block days all the time (morning, afternoon and evening), but they have to work when family and friends are relaxing and can only take time off during the day when most social groups are normally working. Any hobbies have to be solitary (most ministers don't have any). Unlike others they cannot spend weekends visiting wider family. Ministry, in other words, can be excessively isolating. However, churches commonly don't understand this because they assume the minister's friends are the members of the church. How can the pastor be isolated when interacting with all these people every day?

Added to this, a common observation from many ministry spouses is, 'When we were training, nobody made me aware that many different spheres of my life were about to collapse together. Before we entered ministry my home and home life, job, friends and social life, leisure opportunities and church were all demarcated. Now they have all collapsed together into one thing: church. I have no private life. I no longer experience church as a normal member. I have to help my spouse bear the pastoral burdens. My home is public property. People think I am their channel to the minister if they would rather not express their concerns and criticisms personally. It has even changed the relationship with my friends because now I am the minister's spouse. It is all-consuming.' Part of the problem might be their own unrealistic expectations or naivety, but structural and cultural issues related to unrealistic expectations and badly defined roles are also common.

Ministers feel a sense of responsibility to God to work hard, and an inability to challenge expectations from the church that are excessively isolating and consuming. They are expected to be the centre of community for everyone else, but are often the least able to access nourishing community for themselves. They encourage other people in family and community life while starved of it themselves. Those who feed others are often the least well fed. Just ask any church whether they can name who is feeding and nourishing the people who feed them. Most can't.

It is rare for churches to have strong teams of people who share responsibility for pastoral care, so too great a load often falls on paid leaders with the result that their workload perpetually feels unrelenting and infinite. Congregations almost always underestimate how long it takes to do things or how much it is reasonable to expect, meaning that many ministers work at least a day a week more than anyone else thinks they work, week in week out.[2] One minister described it as being expected to be infinitely elastic. It is also quite common for them to be comparatively poorly remunerated but

2 See, for example, Peter Brain, *Going the Distance: How to Stay Fit for a Lifetime of Ministry* (Kingsford, NSW: Matthias Media, 2004), 17.

among the largest donors in percentage terms, which only increases the sense that they and their families are expected to exemplify a sacrificial level of commitment that others don't share.

I am not for one second suggesting that other occupations don't experience very high pressures, but I *am* saying that many ministers and families feel there is an expectation that the church should dominate *all* their time, relationships and resources, leaving no time for any life outside the church context. A large percentage of adverts for ministry jobs are so unrealistic that the angel Gabriel couldn't do them. If candidates agree to these expectations in order to get the job, they are sunk from the outset, because they subsequently have to try to live up to them – or look as though they are. Far from everyone modelling how to live in a wholesome way, leaders start to think that being as pressured and burdened as the most heavily burdened people in the church is the measure of whether they are working enough.

And this is the critical point: they are affirmed and applauded for doing so. Churches deeply admire the sacrificial commitment (that they have required). My counsellor likened these patterns to socially validated self-harm – a complex and self-reinforcing form of self-harm that is easy to fall into and very hard to escape because it is highly approved. Lacking reliable metrics for 'successful' work, social approval becomes an extremely significant motivator, while social disapproval in a close community is devastating.

The other key factor to social approval or disapproval in the minds of many church leaders is an appearance of moral uprightness. They can't appear to struggle with sin; that is for other people. They can even feel they are the only ones in the church whose jobs and homes – let alone being considered worthy leaders – depend on a convincing veneer of perpetual victory over sin. They are forced into dishonesty for the church to feel it has the right kind of moral role models. This has the effect of ensuring leaders find it harder than anyone else in the church to confess sin, or admit to weakness, doubt or struggles with holiness. They feel they are the only ones who are unable to access the same help in these areas that they provide to everyone else.

Of course, having applauded leaders for sham sinlessness, and service that has only been possible through their sacrifice of family, friendship and all external life and relationships, it is all but impossible for followers to say no when the same expectations are turned back on them. Destructive and unsustainable patterns are thereby normalized not just for the leaders, but for the church as a whole. Domineering control might not start intentionally, therefore. It can be created through churches having unrealistic expectations of leaders, which the leaders then transfer back on to the church.

Dominating leaders may feel that the expectations they impose on others do not originate from them, but from the church. Where leaders feel that they and their families are expected to make sacrifices that others are not prepared to share, this can also contain a component of resentment. But more commonly it is about leaders creating what they think the church expects them to create, or sharing an unsustainable burden that has been placed upon them.

Add to all this an evangelistic burden for the lost (people will go to hell if we don't give our all to this church community, under these leaders) and the expectations become completely intolerable. There is no more powerful and horrific a way to manipulate any disciple of Jesus than the suggestion that lack of total life commitment to the church, mission and leaders is responsible for damnation.

It is all rounded off when the most senior leaders are highly capable, 'high-capacity' people. Forceful and forthright personalities, they can appear to sustain carrying many burdens, demands and expectations that in reality damage them, and should never have been shouldered in the first place. Chuck DeGroat perceptively notes that this may well be driven more by the need to bolster vulnerable egos than by servanthood:

> The narcissistic pastor must live in a constant state of ego inflation. The long, hard work of building one thing comes with many disappointments, and thus is inherently ego deflating . . . Proposing and starting multiple things allows the narcissistic pastor to receive all the praise for the successes, and blame 'incompetent staff' for any failures.[3]

When such leaders insist that everyone else be similarly committed, expectations of whole-life participation, unsustainable burdens and moral perfection domino through the culture of the entire church.

3 An affection-needy culture

One final point to note about unhealthy church cultures is that leaders who find ways to make peace with them are often highly emotionally needy. They get all their affirmation from the church. Unhealthy churches can be affirming places when everything is going well, but become particularly difficult when criticism and opposition arise, as there is no escape from it, or other spheres of life to blunt the edge.

To enjoy the affirming environment, or to mitigate the critical one, the temptation is to people-please, possibly also sacrificing home life to maintain approval at church. When this happens, spouses and families are disrespected and dishonoured. The restlessness and anxiety that circulate around the need for affection at church cross over to home, family and marriage.

Needy leaders become manipulating leaders

None of this is intended at all to excuse abuse of position and power. It is simply to recognize that abusers sometimes arise within a destructive context in which their personal moral failings are not the only factor. It sometimes turns out with hindsight that bullies have

---

3 Chuck DeGroat, *When Narcissism Comes to Church: Healing Your Community from Emotional and Spiritual Abuse* (Illinois: IVP, 2020), 78.

themselves been bullied, and that their behaviour is the product of abusive patterns that have previously been modelled to them. Some cultures inadvertently encourage misuse of position through creating unsustainable expectations and conditions for leaders, and via them for everyone.

A church that keeps leaders perpetually anxious, destroys their contentment or squeezes out their spiritual life will create needy leaders. This encourages them to try soothing themselves, meeting their need by controlling their circumstances and environment, or by indulging in secret sins. When abusers are exposed, it is common to put it down to them simply being wicked people. The church can sidestep uncomfortable questions about itself by placing all the blame at the feet of the individual: 'This person was just a lone bad apple, definitely not symptomatic of a toxic paradigm in the church.' This conveniently avoids the need to examine the church culture that allowed the leader to abuse, or that created the conditions within which to become abusive.

Leaders who are otherwise well intentioned might begin to want increased power and authority, then, out of feeling perpetually overburdened and anxious. This may be especially true in churches where the ecclesiological assumption is that the responsibility of 'laity' is to support trained and ordained clergy in *their* mission (an almost exact inversion of the Ephesians 4 pattern of leaders equipping everybody else).

Toxic paradigms

Once a leader has managed to gain decisive control over all authority mechanisms, those structures become self-referencing and self-sustaining. They become stable.

Defaults are habitual and assumed beliefs and actions that people in organisations rely on for stability and predictability.

'Defaults are the ways of looking at situations that lead people to behave in ways that are comfortable and that have generated desirable results in the past.' Defaults have worked well over time.[4]

There are many benefits to stable and predictable church life, but one distinct disadvantage is that there is very little incentive to critically examine it, especially the leaders. Nor is it anyone's job to do so. A church culture that is stable *and* transparent constrains leaders in the legitimate and healthy categories. A culture that is stable but *not* transparent lets them do what they want and rushes to defend them when the need arises, for the very sake of stability. Systemic problems become embedded over a long period, often only coming to light when it becomes obvious that something catastrophic needs to be dealt with. By that point the issue is probably not just the sin of the leader, but the dysfunction of the whole apparatus.

As the authors of *A Church Called Tov* rightly point out, what a pastor or leadership team does first when an allegation is brought against a leader reveals whether the culture of the church is toxic:

If the response is confession and repentance, or a commitment to finding the truth if all the facts are not yet known, that church probably has a healthy . . . culture. On the other hand, if the pastor's first instinct is denial, some form of story or narrative about 'what really happened,' or a defensive posture against 'those who would attack our church or ministry,' there are toxic elements at work within that church's culture.[5]

---

4 Burns, Chapman and Guthrie, *The Politics of Ministry*, 99, quoting Heifetz, Grashow and Linsky.
5 Scot McKnight and Laura Barringer, *A Church Called Tov: Forming a Goodness Culture that Resists Abuses of Power and Promotes Healing* (Illinois: Tyndale House Publishers, 2020), 41.

I have proposed the Five Stages of the slippery slope as a conceptual framework for understanding how power and position come to be misused. The steps also suggest further evaluative questions to help discern whether leadership practice is moving in a healthy or toxic direction. I have provided a more detailed and specific list in the accompanying online resource, *Audit of Abuse of Power*, available at <https://ivpbooks.com/powerful-leaders>.

The important thing is for church officers to become organization-ally more self-aware regarding questions of power, and to be clear about how any concerns can be handled in a godly fashion. They are responsible for independent and transparent investigations pro-ceeding from biblical principles, to avoid conflicts of interest and hold people to account.

They are also the guardians of the healthy policies, procedures and codes of practice that characterize a healthy organizational culture. A church officer reading this will reasonably want to know how we can actually identify behaviour that is being intentionally concealed. Abusive leaders are good at concealment. Manipulative, deceitful leaders commonly indemnify themselves against questioning by being winsome, while the brutal leader does so by appealing to apparent successes.

Some key issues to explore that might reveal whether leaders are either misusing their power or at risk of doing so, or that church practices and culture place you at risk include:[6]

---

6   See also the questions in the accompanying resource *Audit of Abuse of Power*.

- Does your church culture value the accountability, plurality and transparency for leaders explored in this book? Structures and policies alone are insufficient without a healthy culture behind them. Is this reflected in structures and policies? If so, how? If not, where are the gaps?
- Do people in your church care enough if structures and policies have been violated to take action to enforce them? Or would that be perceived as too damaging or threatening? If so, they are worthless.
- Are your policies, procedures, boundaries and codes of best practice clear and robust enough that they could be used to investigate the most senior leaders? Or could abusive leaders find ways to evade such scrutiny through controlling systems or by use of their relational capital?
- Relatively speaking, does your church culture make it easy or hard for a leader to repent?
- What would happen if a trusted member or church officer expressed concerns about misuse of power by the minister? Are you confident that you have mechanisms for concerns to be received in a healthy way? If not, what underlies your lack of confidence?
- What does accountability and review look like for the most senior leaders, in practice? Are you confident that they are appropriately accountable for their use of authority?
- Would your team be likely to recognize if the leadership culture in the church had been hijacked? And if they did, would they be more likely to acknowledge it or to abdicate responsibility?
- Does your church seem to lose or fire staff or volunteer leaders too frequently? Is the role of senior leaders in this ever scrutinized?

- Do the most senior leaders actively help the church put provisions in place that are strong enough to be applied to them, if the need were to arise?
- Is there anything in the leadership of your church that you are allowing, excusing or defending because it would be too difficult or painful to examine or challenge it?
- Does your church have a policy whereby, as a last resort, leaders could be disqualified and removed? The threshold for activation of this should always be high, but leaders who cannot be removed are in much greater danger of exceeding their authority simply because they can carry on trying until they succeed.
- In your church is it anyone's responsibility to consider these issues?

Good governance

I have made the point that clear principles, policies, procedures and codes of best practice are important factors in ensuring leadership is done in the light, not least because leaders gain trust mainly in relational ways that are less open to scrutiny. They are core to transparent good governance. We cannot simply assume leaders are walking in the light if relationships are the only evidence we rely on. Ensuring clarity and scrutiny in these areas boosts organization-level trustworthiness and confidence, and provides the means to hold leaders to account in ways that personal relationships cannot.

Policies define good practice and help to keep everyone honest. Of particular relevance to issues of leadership, authority and power are those concerning:

- the nature and extent of leadership roles and authority;
- the operation of teams, especially mutual expectations regarding accountabilities and responsibilities between senior

and junior staff, and between paid leaders and unpaid elders or equivalents;

- safeguarding, and how accountability works between safeguarding officers and ministers/elders;
- leader reviews, including frequency, regularity and areas to be covered (this could be upwards in denominational structures, downwards to church members, or collegially with elders, church wardens or peers);
- electronic communication and social media;
- conflict of interests;
- expectations on volunteers;
- expenses;
- disciplinary matters, including dismissal processes;
- grievance issues;
- whistle-blowing.

Is your church wearing its seatbelt?

Procedures, policies and protocols, implemented in transparent and collegially accountable ways, are the seatbelt that allows you to drive the car of church ministry quickly but safely. They mitigate power imbalances by putting limitations on the over-reach of leadership authority. They provide consistent, well-advertised approaches to the use of power that are objective and not controlled by the leaders. Boundaries are not intended as constraints but as safeguards. They can never absolutely guarantee ethical behaviour but can reduce the risk of temptation by making sure that wrongdoing is more easily visible. It is useful to accompany all of these with regularly reviewed codes of best practice that explain shared values and commitments to living and leading in the light.

Churches that lack accountability structures for leaders (or where leaders have dismantled them) are powerless when things go wrong. Not only are they driving without a seatbelt, they have cut the brakes and may be hurtling towards a cliff. Merely having governance structures doesn't necessarily improve things if they aren't strong enough. An obvious example is when safeguarding or accountability for the conduct of the minister is vested in a single individual who will personally become deeply vulnerable if an accusation needs to be brought. These things need to be handled by a group of trusted people if there is to be confidence that the most senior leaders can be brought to account.[7] This protects:

- the most senior leaders from themselves (they being most at risk of misusing power);
- leaders from mischievous accusations from troublemakers;
- other people from leaders;
- the safeguarding officer from becoming the focus for spurious accusations against leaders, from conflicts between leaders and members, and from the most senior leaders when those leaders go wrong.

Healthy church culture

Churches and church officers of all kinds need to be educated about these things if they wish to create a healthily transparent environment that is open to honest self-evaluation. But most important is the culture of the church. It is rightly said that culture eats process for breakfast. A condemning culture that makes repentance hard leads to everyone covering up and pretending to be sinless, leaders most of all. In such a culture they build up defensive layers and masks even before their leadership trespasses into the illegitimate categories. If the church culture makes it impossible for leaders to confess, repent and receive forgiveness at Stages 1 and 2, they can't and won't when they get to Stage 3.

---

7 The caveat to this is that under normal circumstances such a group is accountable to appointed leaders. The relationship between the two needs to be very carefully defined.

Leading in repentance

Lastly, when leaders repent, other church officers will have the responsibility of helping them in their brokenness and sin, the church in its pain and need to take action, and any specific victims they have damaged or traumatized.

In a private conversation, a denominational leader lamented to me that disciplinary processes in his denomination were unconcerned about victims and only about financial irregularity, safeguarding breaches or public scandal. And even in those cases it was concerned about reputation management rather than the suffering that an abusive leader had caused in the church. Perhaps the clearest example of tribes protecting themselves at the expense of victims is when disgraced leaders are able to resign, only to be reappointed quietly in new roles elsewhere without sanction, discipline or repentance. When this happens, it sends a dreadful signal that the worst consequences of abusing your position aren't really that bad.

Churches, under the direction of their officers, cannot allow this. Church officers are responsible for exposing wrong and standing with the wronged. Their concern is spiritual healthiness and repentance, not defending the reputation of the system or of individual leaders. Avoidance or pushing things under the carpet for the sake of survival or reputation is not only culpably wicked, it further wounds victims. If people have been mistreated and tried to report it but had their concerns ignored, it effectively discredits them in addition to their other wounds. This can easily destroy their faith in the church, leaders and maybe even God.

It is right and biblical that leaders have protections. The work of ministry is always open to complaints and accusations that are misled, incorrect, untrue or mischievous. I know settings where church officers have done everything they possibly can by way of good process and transparent scrutiny, but have nevertheless been extensively criticized because they haven't delivered the verdict a complainant wanted. Perhaps the most that can be hoped for in such circumstances is that the officers are able to fully present the process to the church to show that everything was conducted properly, even though not everyone is satisfied.

Everyone is entitled to due process and presumption of innocence while allegations are tested and examined. Of course, this applies to those bringing accusations as well as to the accused. As we have seen it is usually costly for someone to challenge a leader. It is important to suspend judgement until the process is complete. However, leaders *must not* be protected at *all* costs. Churches must never be places that are stacked in favour of the powerful.

Needless to say, these are not matters that controlling or abusive leaders – or even those accused of being so – can have any hand in steering, regardless of any repentance on their part; it is crucial for them to submit to the guidance and shepherding of others.

Spotting danger signs is hard. When everyone is going with the flow, we often don't even realize the flow is there. Legitimate authority gets corroded imperceptibly by degrees, the key factor being lack of openness to scrutiny. Manipulative leaders move from confidentiality to privacy and then to secrecy. When they actively try to ensure they can't be observed – or even if there is a suspicion they might be doing so – it is no longer possible to say with confidence that 'we have renounced secret and shameful ways; we do not use deception, nor do we distort the word of God. On the contrary, by setting forth the truth plainly we commend ourselves to every man's conscience in the sight of God' (2 Corinthians 4:2).

12

What next for cultures and tribes?

These are the words of the Amen, the faithful and true witness, the ruler of God's creation. I know your deeds, that you are neither cold nor hot. I wish you were either one or the other! So, because you are lukewarm – neither hot nor cold – I am about to spit you out of my mouth. You say, 'I am rich; I have acquired wealth and do not need a thing.' But you do not realise that you are wretched, pitiful, poor, blind and naked. I counsel you to buy from me gold refined in the fire, so that you can become rich; and white clothes to wear, so that you can cover your shameful nakedness; and salve to put on your eyes, so that you can see.

(Revelation 3:14–18)

What are cultures and how do they go wrong?

Finally, we must consider what happens when wider Christian cultures and tribes go wrong and stand in need of reform. Many concerns are being raised among British and American evangelicals about the extent to which certain evangelical cultures have either enabled or covered up for abusive individual leaders. However, cultures can be nebulous things. Just as corporations have been described as 'an ingenious device for obtaining profit without individual responsibility',[1] in a similar way cultures promote narratives,

---

1 Ambrose Bierce quotes, *The Devil's Dictionary/The Cynic's Word Book*, 1906.

attitudes and group codes and behaviours that no single individual can be said to be responsible for. Or, in fact, that all individuals can disclaim responsibility for.

Cultures are shared attitudes and habits – 'the way we do things around here'. More formally, we can define a culture as a social-plausibility structure created by shared narratives, goals, methods, attitudes, spoken and unspoken codes, relationships, friendships, patrons, meeting places and bubbles or echo chambers. While most people can identify certain concrete features of a culture, such as shared meeting places or key individuals, they are just as much about shared intuitions, instincts and experiences, and diaphanous networks of connections.

While nebulous, at the same time cultures really shape us. Everyone in a culture knows how the narratives and codes work, and how they shape what is expected, said, done and thought. Everyone knows who is at the top table, even though they may have no formal position or title. Adherence to the narrative is the price of entry; promoting the narrative is the membership fee for continuing to belong. Hence those who identify with a culture define it according to features they appreciate and relate to, while dismissing those aspects that don't sit quite right as an aberration or not foundational to what the culture is like. Shared values and narratives create a high degree of social cohesiveness, but these can turn into groupthink that results in a deterioration in critical examination.

Of course, this doesn't have to be the case. A main difference between healthy, shared cultural values and groupthink is the ability to listen and a desire for reformability, which internally embeds self-examination and externally welcomes outside critical friends. I'm grateful for an insightful observation from Caleb Woodbridge, that a healthy culture is like a biological cell in that it is semi-permeable. It can take in positive outside influences while filtering out influences that are harmful. Or, to change the illustration, it is like an immune system that damages the health of the body if it is either over-protective or under-functioning.[2]

It has been said that 'Every great cause begins as a movement, becomes a business, and eventually degenerates into a racket'.[3] What starts as vibrant and positive fossilizes by degrees when it becomes inaccessible to critical examination. In the process it first loses self-awareness, then becomes impervious to critique and finally unreformable. Perhaps the process may go a little like this:

1 *A cause is identified.* Shared goals, experiences and commitments are established.
2 *A network develops.* It has a group mentality, common narrative, friendship groups, entry criteria, meeting places, methodologies and even common language. These become the repository of shared cultural values.
3 *The narrative becomes the most influential thing.* It is the culture's self-understanding, the way it describes itself and the important strategic nature of its work to itself and others. The narrative may be susceptible to exaggeration. There is an inbuilt tendency in the human heart to want to see ourselves as better than we really are.
4 *A vital part of the narrative is that the culture is us.* We are now part of a self-perpetuating family of patronage where we have each other's backs. We have a network that we can rely on, perhaps that will find us ministry positions and guarantee our security.
5 *The narrative creates an in-group and an out-group.* The narrative defines who is seen as mature, effective, strategic, reliable, sound or awesome (pick the self-congratulatory adjective that best fits your culture!). By an amazing coincidence, it is the ones who are within the culture and

---

2 In personal conversation.
3 Eric Hoffer, *The Temper of Our Time* (Bucaneer Books, 1976).

who buy into the narrative! The more faithfully you adhere to it and the better you are at employing the methods and tools of the culture, the more power and prestige it is likely to apportion to you.

6 *The price of critiquing the culture grows.* This would mean turning your back on your family and its benefits. Critiquing the narrative means you are no longer seen as mature, effective, etc. When we go as far as to confuse our culture and narrative with the *gospel*, anyone who critiques it is now suspected of not being a believer.

7 *Dependency on the culture creates wilful blindness.* Once inside, there are strong incentives to carry on believing the narrative and to cast a blind eye to things that might undermine it. We become highly invested in certain things being true and certain other things not being true – even more so when the culture and narrative are undergirding organizations and salaries, pensions and reputations, and when legacies depend on not rocking the boat. We are essentially forced to remain a part of the team and to continue to express enthusiasm we may not feel because we can't expose the flaws in something on which we are deeply dependent. Disloyalty might even result in loss of livelihood.

8 *Wilful blindness becomes genuine blindness.* The more we choose to turn a blind eye, the less able we become to see the reality of the culture. Our wilful blindness causes us to receive external critique or criticism as rivalry, confirmation of the correctness of the narrative we have constructed, or as persecution. Complacency and the echo chamber do the rest.

Culture is collective, attitudinal, conforming and hard to escape. The quote from Laodicea at the start of the chapter shows how it is possible to end up spiritually blind and impoverished while believing we are far-seeing and well resourced.

The central conforming feature is not some grand structure that can be held to account, regularly evaluated and reviewed, but rather the narrative, group mentality and not wanting to forsake its benefits or longstanding friendship with those who hold to it unquestioningly. This explains why cultures can be incredibly powerful and intangible at one and the same time. If a culture also becomes inseparable from unaccountable main leaders, such that they promote it and it provides cover for them, it is next to impossible to correct, for that would require insight from outside the culture, which is deemed inadmissible by the very fact that it is external.

In The Emperor's New Clothes, the reason the townspeople self-censored and refused to call time on the fraud was that the wilfully blind, self-evidently naked and foolish person was the emperor. You don't question or embarrass the emperor! He doesn't have to force individuals to comply – they will do so anyway, because everyone does. As we have seen in the case of individual leaders, the more power a culture acquires, and the more apparently successful it becomes, the harder it is for anyone to dissent, regardless of how obvious the faults and failings are. And the apparent successes may be considerable. A church or movement may experience many people being converted, baptized and discipled. This genuine spiritual fruit can continue for a time within a culture that is becoming toxic in other ways. However, we must never downplay, ignore or excuse coercive patterns of leadership by pointing to the good that particular leaders or ministries have done. It may be the case, but that is beside the point.

Where too much is at stake to allow something to fail, cultural self-regulation, if it exists at all, is unlikely to be self-critical. Challenge the narrative, codes or doctrines of your tribe and you probably won't be able to lead or remain in it any more. Groupthink culture shuts dissenters down. Hence cultures become impervious to change and reform until something terrible becomes unavoidably public – for example, the exposure of the moral failing or coercive practice of a high-profile leader. By which point there may have been years of abuse and trauma behind the scenes, and other stories and victims that will never come to light because they don't involve someone famous.

Cultures can be tremendously effective refuges for denialists, because they transfer responsibility from specific issues and identifiable individuals on to the collective mass. When disaster strikes and obvious questions are asked about whether the culture or culture leaders have been an enabling factor, everyone can claim plausible deniability: maybe the culture has gone wrong, but in ways that could only be seen with hindsight; unless specific individual sins can be pointed out, for which specific leaders or groups may repent, there isn't a case to answer. Nobody takes responsibility and no-one is specifically held responsible. However, neither is the culture or narrative, because to blame the collective would be to tarnish innocent people, and the good achieved by the culture, along with the guilty.

This is to entirely miss the point. Cultural degeneracy isn't just about specific sins or specific false teachings, but about attitudes, narratives and self-perpetuating hegemony, which are themselves corrupted and corrupting, but less easy to identify.

Cultures and the behaviour of sinful leaders

It is easy when a leader falls into sin to assume a direct causal relationship between what they have done and the narratives – and possibly the theology – of the culture with which they identify. Because culture tends not to be transparent it is easy to implicate it when leaders are found to have acted non-transparently: 'It's not just that individual, it's the whole lot of them!'

But things are never that easy. For every abusive leader there will probably be a lot more who aren't. Is the culture responsible for the bad ones but not the good? Is it that the bad ones embraced and lived out the culture while the good ones somehow resisted its wicked impulses? Or is it the good ones who exemplify the culture and the bad ones who are the aberration? Being wounded and traumatized by abusive leaders doesn't, in itself, reveal whether the culture or tribe of which they are a part is a material enabling factor. After all, abusive leadership is found in a wide variety of organizational cultures and contexts, from Hollywood (as shown by the MeToo movement) to politics and the business world, as well as church contexts. The enabling cultural weaknesses will vary from situation to situation and the exact abusive leadership patterns will differ depending on the culture in which they occur, but those in each culture have a responsibility to address their shortcomings.

In fact, there are a number of possible relationships between the culture and an abusive leader, qualified by whether a culture is:

- actively safeguarding against the potential for coercive leadership;
- inactive and not regularly taking steps to review, thereby potentially enabling it at least by blindness and omission.

In the first case it may still go wrong despite proactive actions by culture leaders to make it impossible for an abusive leader to exist within it. Someone finds a way to contravene the safeguards despite their best efforts.

In the second case there are several possibilities:

- The culture is not intentionally enabling. The coercive leader manipulates and acts in contravention of the culture. But the culture isn't actively *disabling*, because it hasn't taken proactive steps to make it impossible or at least less likely.
- There are identifiable features of the culture that may be enabling factors which attract abusive leaders, make abusive

behaviour and leadership styles more possible or likely, or provide cover for abusive leaders.

- There is an inseparable relationship between the culture and the abusive leader because they have either created it, control it or hold an unquestionable position within it.

Sadly, it usually takes issues of power abuse to cause a culture to take a long hard look at itself, by which time a great deal of harm has been done. But examining these things when a scandal comes to light is extremely difficult because of the inevitable incendiary climate. By the time someone is willing to blow the whistle on cultural sins, they may themselves already be mired in layers of complicity. They know that as soon as they call out the emperor's nakedness they will become the enemy not only of their own tribe, but perhaps also of victims, who think they are implicated in the very abuse they are exposing. Nobody wants to bring down a firestorm on their own head. It is hard to speak out for truth and integrity if doing so will immediately expose someone to accusations of complicity in pastoral bullying, or worse. They may feel that they are walking on eggshells, when anything they say which is nuanced or conciliatory will be interpreted as minimizing sin or victim-blaming. This is complicated even further when a leader may bear a degree of responsibility for things going wrong but is also a victim. Hence, the exposure is delayed, with fear overcoming integrity until the pain of not acting outweighs the danger of doing so.

A crucial indicator of whether there is a soft-hearted and penitent attitude is someone's first instinct. Is it to listen to victims, search the heart and seek objective external evaluation; to repent and make restitution? Or is it to self-defensively circle the wagons and come out all guns blazing? A crisis may have the silver lining of sifting the tender-hearted and repentant from the brutal.

With the benefit of greater distance from a presenting crisis, other questions can be explored:

- Can it be documented that leaders within a culture took proactive steps to ensure spiritual healthiness, transparency and robust safeguarding within that culture before a crisis arose?
- Are culture leaders interested in investigation of the culture, or are they invested in denying anything could be wrong?
- Does the culture value spiritual formation and prayerfulness? Or is it dominated by activities, size-metrics and skills development?
- Has the culture reached such a threshold of influence that challenging from inside will be viewed with suspicion or hostility, and challenge from outside has become impossible? This is especially tempting when you are attacked from outside by those who aren't Christians or have substantial theological differences to you, but this begs another question, which is whether the culture identifies itself and its survival too closely with the success or failure of the gospel.
- Is the culture in practice inseparable from its main leaders?
- Does the culture believe, or even say, that it is the only real expression of faithful Christianity?
- Does the culture use its apparent successes to argue that it has a monopoly on what the Holy Spirit is doing?
- Are we tempted to use the good things achieved by our culture to balance out, qualify or excuse sinfulness? Worse still, do we use them to exaggerate blessing and make sinfulness seem proportionately less important?
- Are other orthodox believers dismissed out of hand as 'not evangelical enough', or not visionary enough, not teaching well enough, or lacking the Holy Spirit, without speaking to them? If we dismiss people without offering to help them first, it is commonly a mechanism for promoting ourselves. If we can compare the best of our self-image with the worst that we can impute to others, we always look good in our own eyes.

- Are we boastful and proud about what we have created? Are we given to self-congratulation or humility? Does our culture appreciate the name it has made for itself? Remember the people at Babel in Genesis 11 making a name for themselves, compared with Abram in Genesis having God make a name for him.
- Has appropriate honouring of leaders tipped over into inappropriate adulation or idolizing them? Does this make key figures immune from scrutiny by dint of their culture leadership?
- Do we receive external critique automatically as jealousy, rivalry, immaturity or false teaching, simply because it comes from people who are not one of us?
- When sin is revealed, is the instinct of our culture to issue corporate apologies that seem to victims to be an insincere way to avoid individuals taking personal responsibility?
- Is the culture used to justify and support suspiciously large salaries? Are finances transparent?
- Would a scandal ever cause us to close a ruined ministry? Or does the culture provide sufficient cover to allow it to continue with minor changes and the same leaders?

Enabling cultures?

Questions like these reveal our cultural instinct. Are we constantly reforming our culture for the sake of spiritual healthiness and holiness? Or are we constantly perpetuating culture for the sake of continuity and the benefit of individuals within it? Will the response to crisis be to seek and welcome fresh thinking about repentance and healthiness? Or will the dark side of corporate responsibility ensure that nobody speaks out? Will we let God challenge our attitudes, or will it just be business as usual and put all the blame on lone bad apples?

Are we part of an enabling culture? It is a hard question to consider until something goes wrong. But much easier are: what is the best we can do to ensure we are less in danger of becoming an enabling culture? What safeguards do we need? What mechanisms for people to raise concerns and be heard safely? What principles should be in place for how high-profile culture leaders respond in the event of a scandal? What would repentance at the level of culture look like? Should high-profile leaders ever consider stepping out of culture leadership in the light of cultural failings?[4] Or do we assume we must hold on to influence, either with the honourable motive of putting our own house in order, or with the more suspect assumption that only we are in a position to correct things? Do we *need* to be important people? Are we willing, humbly, to stop doing things? Where can we find external, critical friends who can help us? And how may we walk in repentance and faith? If we want to be always reforming, these things are vital.

Healthy cultures

What is your culture known for? What makes it attractive to those who are inside or those who want to join? What makes it unattractive to others?

I suggest that the roots of cultural health or ill-health lie with what they wish to be known for, which determines why people want to belong or who can belong. 'You are what you love' (as James K. A. Smith's book title has it) applies not just to individuals but to cultures also. A culture that is known for great outcomes, resources and influence draws people who are attracted by those things and establishes the group mentality, attitudes and narrative around them.

---

4   This is not a simplistic question. It is quite possible to imagine a high-profile leader in a culture that has gone wrong who has worked tirelessly behind the scenes to ameliorate the decline. Without them things would have been even worse and their standing aside may not improve things.

The great danger, once again, is false metrics. If we want to belong because of tangible benefits to ourselves, we might unwittingly embrace unhealthiness as the price of entry. If healthy culture is what we desire, tangible benefits – even ones as important as friendship or correct doctrine – can't be the sole attraction, because they alone don't determine whether a culture is healthy or unhealthy.

Rather, the chief attraction has to be a climate of self-evident, vibrant, grace-filled spiritual healthiness. Can you detect the fragrant aroma of Christ manifested in:

- the fruit of the Holy Spirit;
- prayer;
- humility, weakness and modesty;
- delight in the Lord and his Word;
- a deep appreciation of the grace of God, which then manifests itself in gracious attitudes and behaviour;
- thankfulness;
- the modelling of repentance and forgiveness;
- wisdom;
- honesty;
- transparency;
- accountability;
- the blessing and empowering of others without need for reciprocation;
- success being far less important than godliness;
- leaders who don't *need* to be important culture leaders or have large, widely recognized ministries?

In my experience the cultures that most successfully embrace constant reform prayerfully evaluate regularly whether they believe the Lord wishes them to keep running their various ministries, and aren't afraid or ashamed to stop doing even something that seems outwardly highly successful.

Cultures that lack this instinct are assuming that what God wishes to do in the future is synonymous with what they are currently doing, and with the existing leaders and their protégés. To put it another way, when the survival and perpetuation of a culture becomes one of its chief aims such that it can't stop doing things, it is already starting to fossilize, because it is built on foundations other than those of prayer and godliness.

May the Lord give us insight and help us walk in repentance and faith.

Afterword: The peaceful fruit of righteousness

[The LORD] tends his flock like a shepherd:
He gathers the lambs in his arms
and carries them close to his heart;
he gently leads those that have young.
(Isaiah 40:11)

By this all men will know that you are my disciples, if you love
one another.
(John 13:35)

'I came to your seminar on power and position,' Douglas said. 'I
found the Five Stages helpful and have told my church leadership
team about them. I think the thing they are going to need the most
help with is the fact that they love and admire me. I am so grateful
for that, but it means I can get them to do whatever I want very
easily.

'I have asked them to go away and identify anything in the church,
or in me as the minister, that might put me or the church at risk of
coercive leading. When they report back, we will start praying and
working on it together. We should probably have done it before, but
in day-to-day church life it is hard to find time to pause and consider
whether the way we do things is as healthy as it could be.'

Douglas and his leadership team's instincts are all in the right
direction. The church should be highly encouraged as they take steps
together to overtly and unambiguously embed healthiness and
holiness at the heart of leadership.

My prayer is that this book has helped you think about biblical, spiritual leadership through the lens of Christ-like servanthood, rather than through a worldly lens of big characters wielding power with their impressive strength, or subtle manipulators wielding power through the warmth of their impressive smiles and personal winsomeness.

Success metrics

When we cannot measure what is important, we are tempted to turn what we can measure into what is important. I believe the most common way this happens in Christian leadership is for us to define success in our own terms, according to the visible 'fruit' that we can personally pick (or have picked). This might be the evangelist who defines success by number of converts, the pastor by how positive responses are after a service, the youth leader according to how many come to the group, the student worker according to the number of small groups they run, or the missionary by how difficult and sacrificial their work is compared to that of others. Other metrics include size of congregation, personal affirmation, finance, buildings, invitations to join boards or speak on influential platforms.

None of these are intrinsically bad, but used as metrics they gradually draw us away from our first love. Whatever our preferred measure, when we as leaders self-define 'success' in this way, we can then muster our resources and try to control circumstances and people to deliver according to the self-affirming metric 'This is what fruitfulness looks like, and I am the leader who can implement it for you'. Self-serving leaders never define fruitfulness according to criteria they are unable to deliver.

This is a worldly view of fruitfulness, not a Christian one. It can amount to little more than what Jesus described in Matthew 6:1 as doing 'acts of righteousness before men, to be seen by them'. He warns that those who seek human applause have their reward in full but won't be rewarded by God. Underlying are issues of my worth or my legacy. What have *I* done; how am *I* deserving; to what can I point to show that I have been a success? Jamin Goggin and Kyle Strobel put it like this:

> For Christians, the journey into true power begins with the realization of our desire for false power. This hunger for false power is not unique to the pastoral vocation, but is something we all are tempted by whether we are salespeople or stay-at-home moms. In our own ways, we long for validation, recognition, and significance.[1]

When this longing is embraced within a church or wider Christian culture, leaders may feel compelled to keep delivering the visible product that people expect. And then they may be tempted to abuse their position and power to keep the 'fruit' flowing. As one leader said to me: 'I don't get any prizes for standing still.'

Compare this to the missionaries in Asia who said to me, 'We will be obscure, totally unsung, perhaps not successful in our lifetimes but maybe opening up the way for those in the next generation. Jesus is building his church; we want to be in on that. We want to hear "Well done, good and faithful servant" – and that's enough.'

Real fruitfulness is what Jesus produces in us as we abide in him: 'I am the vine; you are the branches. If a man remains in me and I in him, he will bear much fruit; apart from me you can do nothing' (John 15:5).

Jesus' fruit is variously described as the peaceful fruit of righteousness (Philippians 1), a harvest of righteousness (Hebrews 12; James 3), fruit in keeping with repentance (Luke 3) and, most descriptively, the fruit of the Holy Spirit (Galatians 5). Fruitfulness

---

1 Jamin Goggin and Kyle Strobel, *The Way of the Dragon or the Way of the Lamb: Searching for Jesus' Path of Power in a Church that Has Abandoned It* (Thomas Nelson, 2021), 22.

starts with repentance and receiving the Holy Spirit. It abounds in love, discernment and purity. It fills and transforms our characters, by the power of the Holy Spirit, so that we imitate Jesus and enjoy the reality that his righteousness is given to us as a free gift of God's grace. Most importantly, apart from Jesus we can do *nothing at all.*

This fruit removes the need to perform for approval and hence draws out the poison of the desire for power. It engenders a culture of vulnerability, weakness, openness and repentance, flowing from a deep appreciation of the grace of God to sinners. Rules and regulations cannot produce this. The antidote to a culture of self-promoting leaders is one where leaders – and everyone else – repent often and forgive often, delighting themselves in the Lord, praying and praising him for the glory of his wonderful grace. A culture, therefore, in which leaders can lead out of weakness, no longer needing to be impressive or having to prove themselves to receive praise and affirmation from people. Praise God, his grace is sufficient for us!

> To keep me from becoming conceited because of these surpassingly great revelations, there was given me a thorn in my flesh, a messenger of Satan, to torment me. Three times I pleaded with the Lord to take it away from me. But he said to me, 'My grace is sufficient for you, for my power is made perfect in weakness.' Therefore I will boast all the more gladly about my weaknesses, so that Christ's power may rest on me. That is why, for Christ's sake, I delight in weaknesses, in insults, in hardships, in persecutions, in difficulties. For when I am weak, then I am strong.
> (2 Corinthians 12:7–10)

Appendix:
A note on the terminology
of 'spiritual abuse'

The term 'spiritual abuse' has been used in academic circles in the UK for around a decade and has recently become more common currency in the light of abuse scandals. Common usage suggests the category involves patterns of emotional or psychological control through coerced behaviours over a period of time in a religious context. What makes it 'spiritual' is a religious context (for example, a relationship, church, camp, etc.) and the presence of specifically religious features. These include religious justifications or defences for behaviour, (mis)use of religious texts, doctrines being used as tools for control, claims to divine inspiration, or misuse of God's name and/or Word in the perpetration or justification of mistreatment. It is not hard to see the value of the language, especially for giving victims and survivors of abuse a descriptive category to help understand and process their experience and trauma.

However, keen-eyed readers will have spotted that I haven't used this term in the book. I remain personally cautious about it, without wanting to undermine the reality of the phenomena it is trying to describe. My concern centres around the danger of the term being used as a broad catch-all shorthand that conflates a wide range of possible issues. Some of these may constitute abuse, others might not, the only uniting factor being some claim about spiritual authority in a religious setting. I believe that where there are claims of abuse, the categories under which they are investigated need to be as clear as possible, especially in legal contexts. Respected bodies who are all deeply concerned about abuse find they cannot agree on definitions in this case.[1]

There is a risk that anything someone doesn't like or strongly disagrees with in a Christian context can be labelled spiritual abuse – for example, teaching on sin, repentance, hell or the need for salvation, or demonstrably non-abusive use of leadership authority and pastoral practices. Moreover, it potentially becomes a tool for labelling such things in the very worst possible terms. For example, at the time of writing there are moves in the UK to criminalize orthodox teaching on sexuality, and even pastoral prayer, by calling it a safeguarding issue.[2] Throughout wider society in the UK at the present time the category of 'hate incident' is defined by the perception of someone who believes themselves to have been a victim. It doesn't require a burden of proof or even evidence.[3]

I certainly don't want to give any suggestion of minimizing the importance of addressing underlying realities and problems, or of undermining victims by being cautious about particular terminology. However, my concern is that the combination of unclearly defined terms that may be susceptible to category-creep, and burden of proof falling on the accused to demonstrate they were not abusive, could weaken due process to a worrying degree and is open to manipulation. Not only might lack of clarity spread the net very wide, indicting the innocent along with the guilty, but I believe there

1 Compare, for example, the following reports: Dr Lisa Oakley and Justin Humphreys, 'Understanding Spiritual Abuse in Christian Communities' (CCPAS, 2018) at: <https://thirtyoneeight.org/media/2185/spiritualabusesummarydocument.pdf> and 'Reviewing the discourse of "Spiritual Abuse": Logical Problems & Unintended Consequences' – a report by the Evangelical Alliance Theological Advisory Group (Feb 2018) at: <www.eauk.org/assets/files/downloads/Reviewing-the-discourse-of-Spiritual-Abuse>.
2 See, for example, <www.ozanne.foundation/inter-religious-advisory-board-write-to-sec-of-state-regarding-need-to-ban-conversion-therapy/#_edn2>, accessed 5 June 2021.
3 For examples see: <www.citizensadvice.org.uk/law-and-courts/discrimination/hate-crime/what-are-hate-incidents-and-hate-crime/> and <www.app.college.police.uk/app-content/major-investigation-and-public-protection/hate-crime/responding-to-hate/>.

is a possibility that genuine cases of abuse may be diluted and less noticed if there are many more claims to it, and this won't help real victims.

Bibliography

Further reading

Peter Brain, *Going the Distance: How to Stay Fit for a Lifetime of Ministry* (Kingsford, NSW: Matthias Media, 2004).

Bob Burns, Tasha D. Chapman and Donald C. Guthrie, *The Politics of Ministry: Navigating Power Dynamics and Negotiating Interests* (Westmont, IL: IVP, 2019).

Chuck DeGroat, *When Narcissism Comes to Church: Healing Your Community from Emotional and Spiritual Abuse* (Westmont, IL: IVP, 2020).

Jamin Goggin and Kyle Strobel, *The Way of the Dragon or the Way of the Lamb: Searching for Jesus' Path of Power in a Church that Has Abandoned It* (Nashville, TN: Thomas Nelson, 2021).

Chris Green, *The Gift: How Your Leadership Can Serve Your Church* (London: IVP, 2021).

Diane Langberg, *Redeeming Power: Understanding Authority and Abuse in the Church* (Ada, MI: Brazos Press, 2020).

Scot McKnight and Laura Barringer, *A Church Called Tov: Forming a Goodness Culture that Resists Abuses of Power and Promotes Healing* (Carol Stream, IL: Tyndale House Publishers, 2020).

Mark Meynell, *Wilderness of Mirrors: Trusting Again in a Cynical World* (Grand Rapids, MI: Zondervan, 2015).

Lisa Oakley and Justin Humphreys, *Escaping the Maze of Spiritual Abuse: Creating Healthy Christian Cultures* (London: SPCK, 2019).

Harold Rowdon (ed.), *Church Leaders Handbook* (Carlisle: published for Partnership by Paternoster, 2002).

Paul David Tripp, *Dangerous Calling: The Unique Challenges of Pastoral Ministry* (London: IVP, 2012).

Simon P. Walker, *Leading Out of Who You are: Discovering the Secret of Undefended Leadership* (Manchester: Piquant Editions, 2007).

Some relevant reports

I provide links to these reports because they are all provoking widespread reflection at the time of writing. As well as being important reading, they provide a degree of backdrop to the book. It should be noted that the kinds of issues and the role of leaders examined in them, while all serious, vary considerably. Some involve criminality, others do not.

Dr Lisa Oakley and Justin Humphreys, 'Understanding Spiritual Abuse in Christian Communities' (CCPAS, 2018) at: <https://thirtyoneeight.org/media/2185/spiritualabusesummarydocument.pdf>, accessed 12 October 2021.

'Reviewing the discourse of "Spiritual Abuse": Logical Problems & Unintended Consequences', a report by the Evangelical Alliance Theological Advisory Group (Feb 2018) at: <www.eauk.org/assets/files/downloads/Reviewing-the-discourse-of-Spiritual-Abuse.pdf>, accessed 23 October 2021.

The Crowded House Independent Learning Review, Thirtyone:eight, October 2020 at: <https://thirtyoneeight.org/get-help/independent-reviews/crowded-house-review/>, accessed 12 October 2021.

Independent Lessons Learned Review (incorporating an Audit of Safeguarding Arrangements) Concerning Jonathan Fletcher and Emmanuel Church Wimbledon, Thirtyone:eight, March 2021 at: <https://thirtyoneeight.org/get-help/independent-reviews/jonathan-fletcher-review/>, accessed 12 October 2021.

Investigation reports by the Independent Inquiry into Child Sexual
Abuse at: .

The John Smyth Independent Case Review, Scripture Union,
March 2021, at: <https://content.scriptureunion.org.uk/
js-review>, accessed 12 October 2021.

While not a report in the same way, *Christianity Today*'s podcast
investigation of 'The Rise and Fall of Mars Hill' is also a very
relevant case study at: <www.christianitytoday.com/ct/
podcasts/rise-and-fall-of-mars-hill/>, accessed 12 October 2021.

Living Leadership

GROWING DISCIPLE-MAKING LEADERS

Living Leadership pastors and disciples Christian leaders.

We are a growing network across the UK, Ireland and beyond, united in **helping Christian leaders and their spouses to live joyfully in Christ and serve him faithfully**.

We support leaders and their spouses through:

formation *Training in heart, knowledge, skills and wisdom*

Through courses, seminars, masterclasses, residentials and leadership schools, we provide training on grace-filled leadership, pastoral care, disciple-making, team-building and much more.

refresh *Support for living joyfully and serving faithfully*

Through annual Pastoral Refreshment Conferences, group mentoring, regional Refreshment Days and our online Network, we provide regular and one-off support. Wrapping around this, our Associates offer tailored one-to-one mentoring and pastoral care.

resources *Equipping with quality biblical content and tools*

We produce accessible, biblically faithful tools, resources, videos and podcasts to encourage leaders in lifelong growth. Our toolkits and Codes of Best Practice are available for churches and organizations seeking to raise their standards of leadership and leader care.

Find out more:

www.livingleadership.org

or find us as @livingleaders on most social media platforms